FOCUS
ON CHINA

Values and Religion
in China Today

FOCUS ON CHINA

Values and Religion in China Today

Mary Lou Martin, M.M.

Donald MacInnis, Ph.D.

A MARYKNOLL EDUCATION PROGRAM
WORLD AWARENESS SERIES

MARYKNOLL FATHERS AND BROTHERS
Maryknoll, New York 10545

About the Authors

Donald MacInnis, Ph.D., a sinologist, is the author of *Religious Policy and Practice in Communist China* (Macmillan, 1972).

Mary Lou Martin, M.M., served as a missioner among the Chinese people in Hong Kong for over thirty years, and has also had much experience in preparing educational materials about the Far East.

Credits

Project Director: William O'Connor
Curriculum Advisor: Jane Keegan, RDC
Design and Production: Greg Johnson, ART DIRECTIONS
Research Associate: Susan Perry
Printing: RK Graphics, Inc.

Illustration Credits

A number of the illustrations used in this book are from *Traditional Chinese Cut-Paper Designs* (B. Melchers), and *Treasury of Chinese Design Motifs* (J. D'Addetta), both published by Dover Publications, Inc., Mineola, NY. Other Chinese folk art cut-paper designs have come from various sources originating in the People's Republic of China (artists unknown).

ISBN 0-941395-01-4

Table of Contents

Introduction

**PURPOSE OF
THIS BOOK**

This series of lessons, prepared for secondary school teachers, is designed to supplement the treatment of Chinese and Asian history and culture as it is currently presented in textbooks. None of the standard textbooks reviewed deals in depth with either topic, values or religion.

We believe that American high school students—searching for a faith and values system of their own in a time of rapid social change—will want to know more than standard facts about China's history, culture, politics, and geography. It may surprise them to learn of the struggles, the search for faith and meaning of their student counterparts in China during recent decades of violent social change.

A CRY OF DESPAIR

In 1980, a letter from a despairing young woman, printed in the national magazine *Chinese Youth (Zhongguo Qingnian)*, brought letters from over 40,000 young people in response to her anguished outcry.

> *I am now twenty-three years old. It should be said that for me life has just begun. But it seems that all the mystery and attraction of life no longer exist and I have already reached its end. Looking back on my journey, it has been a trip from crimson to gray, a trip from hope through disappointment to despair, a long river of ideology originating at a selfless source and terminating with the self as center....* *

Pan Xiao, the writer of this now-famous letter, is one of millions of Chinese youth today struggling with a major shift in national goals and values since the death of Mao Zedong and the rise to power of new leaders. What are their goals in life? How do they view the pragmatic "four modernizations" as China's current priorities, in contrast to the Maoist vision for egalitarian sharing and selfless service to neighbors and to the nation? How deeply ingrained is China's ancient heritage of traditional values, culture and religion? Are these carried on today in the family and interpersonal relations, in the revival of religious practice, and in traditional rites for marriages, funerals and festivals?

*Zhongguo Qingnian, 1980, No. 5.

A SEARCH FOR MEANING AND PURPOSE

This series of lessons will introduce American students to China's traditional values and religions, and to the challenges to those traditions due to the impact of the West and the whole range of social change and modernization taking place in China. We will examine the search for meaning and purpose, for national unity, for selfless goals and socialist values promoted during the Cultural Revolution, and the revision of those goals and values since the death of Mao. China's youth today, like their counterparts in the United States, struggle to find personal meaning and commitment in a time of confusion and challenge to traditional values.

CONTENT OVERVIEW

The first two lessons are designed to introduce the topic and to lead American students to reflect on how we form our images of another nation and people—in this case, the Chinese.

Seven lessons are devoted to traditional religions and Christianity in China before 1949, the fate of religion under Communism, the Chinese Marxist views of religion, and the current revival of religious practice following the liberalizing of policies in 1979.

The final four lessons shift from religion to related questions about life and death, meaning and purpose, and the rights of the individual in a crowded nation of over one billion people. Both American and Chinese youth continue to ponder the same basic question: What is the meaning of life?

TEACHING SCHEDULE

The entire set of lessons can be used as a unit of thirty teaching days (six weeks), or certain sections can be chosen to supplement existing textbook material. Combined with lessons from standard textbooks on geography, history and culture, a full semester could be devoted to a comprehensive teaching unit on China. The optional class activities, such as role playing, short dramas, and films, offer flexibility in overall planning.

GOALS

Throughout the lessons, the goal is to stimulate American students to reflect on their own experience, correlating and contrasting it with what they are learning about China. Where standard textbooks present in survey fashion only highlights of Chinese history and culture, the aim of this material is to lead students beyond basic facts to a deeper understanding of the Chinese people with a different values tradition. The struggle of Chinese youth to find meaning and purpose in life is mirrored in the experience of American youth.

METHODOLOGY

This is a teacher's guide, offering suggested lesson outlines, background information, primary source materials, discussion topics, class activities, vocabulary worksheets, short dramas and role playing, and special assignments. A listing of titles and sources for reference books, audio-visuals, and curriculum materials on China is also included in the resources section in the back of the book.

These materials are prepared with two age groups in mind: ninth/tenth graders, and eleventh/twelfth graders. Most of the student activities and special assignments have been classroom tested. Younger students will delight in activities such as role-playing Lord Macartney and the Chinese Emperor, or improvising the one-act play "Do Not Spit at Random." Other assignments and projects will challenge them to self-examination and creative thinking.

A word should be said about romanization of Chinese names and places. We will follow the practice adopted by American publishers, using the *pin-yin* system now used throughout China, except for well-known names and places such as Chiang Kai-shek and Peking which would be unrecognizable to most people in the new spelling (Jiang Jieshi and Beijing).

Because special terms in the Primary Sources may be a problem, especially for the younger students, a vocabulary page is included with each lesson. It is recommended that students keep a vocabulary notebook.

A useful ongoing assignment is to require students to read their daily newspaper and news magazines throughout the study of this unit, clipping or photocopying anything dealing with China. As a final assignment, students might organize and analyze these materials by topic, such as: internal politics, foreign relations, economic development, U.S.–China relations, society and culture, values and religion, and human interest stories.

Social studies teachers can usefully augment this unit by correlating with the English department, asking them to assign the reading of books such as Pearl Buck's *The Good Earth*, which is replete with examples of daily life, social inequities, and peasant misery in the 1930s. More recent books are *Thunder Out of China* by Theodore White and Annalee Jacoby (1946), *Report from a Chinese Village* by Jan Myrdal (1965), *Through Chinese Eyes*, Peter J. Seybolt, editor (1981), and two recent autobiographies by Chinese young people: *Son of Revolution* by Liang Heng and Judith Shapiro (1983) and *Dragon's Village* by Y. T. Chen (1980).

In preparing this curriculum, several social studies teachers with experience teaching about China, curriculum specialists, textbook publishers, China scholars, and school administrators were consulted, including: the Center for Teaching about China of the US–China Peoples Friendship Association, the China Council of the Asia Society, the East Asian Curriculum Project at Columbia University, the Bay Area China Education Project at Stanford University, and the Asian Studies Curriculum Center at New York University. The editorial committee received encouragement and endorsement from CACC (Catholics in America Concerned with China). We are indebted to all consultants, but take sole responsibility for this final product.

The Editorial Committee

LESSON 1

Values Old and New: American Images of China

LESSON PURPOSE

The purpose of this lesson is (**1**) to stimulate reflection on how we form our images of another nation and people, and (**2**) to lead the students to more accurate perceptions of China and the Chinese people.

MAP EXERCISE

Ask students to fill in the blank, line drawing map of China, naming as many rivers, cities and border nations as they can. Duplicate the map on page 8, and distribute it to the class for this exercise.

Display a map of China and its border nations. If possible, use a world map that was printed in China. One can be ordered from China Books & Periodicals, Inc., 2020 24th Street, San Francisco, CA 94110, which will have China in the center, rather than the United States.

QUESTIONNAIRE ABOUT CHINA

Ask the students to give brief answers to these questions. Caution them to answer honestly, without joking, in order to make the class tabulation meaningful. Hand in papers unsigned.

1. What do you think of when you hear the words "China—the country"?

2. What do you think of when you hear the words "China—its people"?

3. What is the approximate population of China today?

4. How big is the land area of China, compared to the United States? Half as large? About the same size? Much larger? (See the map on page 6.)

5. What is the chief religion of China? Name other religions in China.

6. Give the names of two or three Chinese leaders in the twentieth century.

7. Give the names of two or three Chinese cities.

8. What do you value most about the American way of life?

9. How would Chinese students answer the same question about their own way of life?

10. Why should Americans study about China?

Collect and shuffle the questionnaires. Read them together with the class and discuss some of the answers. Explain the meaning of "cultural bias" as it applies to this exercise.

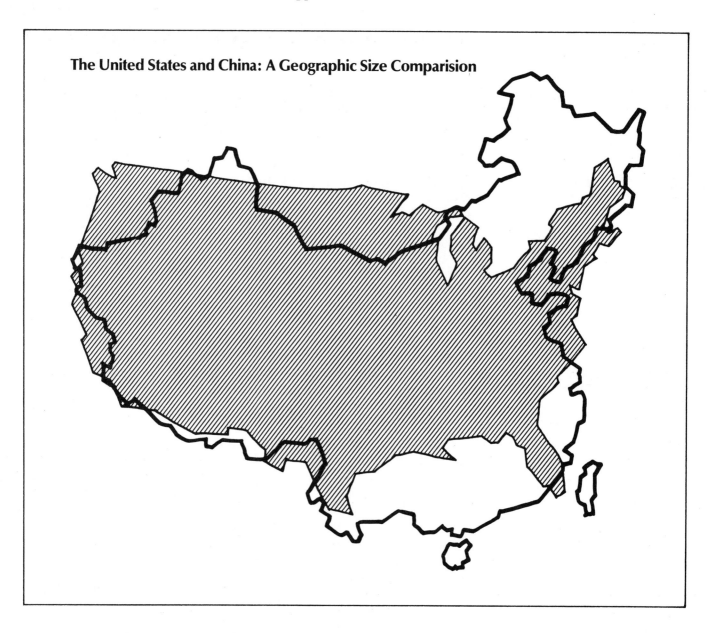

The United States and China: A Geographic Size Comparision

LESSON REVIEW

QUESTIONS FOR DISCUSSION

1. How accurate are these images of China?

2. Why did they answer specific questions as they did?

3. What images do they have of China and the Chinese people?

4. What were their sources of information and perceptions of China?

5. Were their answers influenced by cultural bias?

INTRODUCTION TO CHINA

1. Using the map, discuss the geography of China, how far it is from the United States, how long it takes to get there by plane, by ship, by the old sailing ships. Explain why China *(Zhong-guo)*, meaning "the Middle Kingdom," always saw itself as the center of the universe, and how Chinese civilization was far advanced over Europe's until the decline of the Manchu (Qing) Dynasty in the nineteenth century. Refer to the list of Chinese inventions in Primary Sources, page 88.

2. Summarize the history of China, with particular reference to the impact of the West following the Opium War (1840–1842), the breakdown of traditional values, the collapse of political and social structures in the "century of humiliation" (1840–1949), and the rise of Communism with its own values system. Trace the course of U.S.–China relations during the Cold War Period; note the irony of President Nixon leading the breakthrough in diplomatic relations with China with his trip in 1972.

3. Finally, point out the need for Americans to be better informed about China, as the center of world population and development shifts to Asia.

CLASS ASSIGNMENT

Each student will interview two or three adults, or other students, asking these same questions, using a tape recorder or notebook. They will report their results back in class. The purpose of the activity is to show that even adults are often poorly informed about China, despite its size and importance in the world.

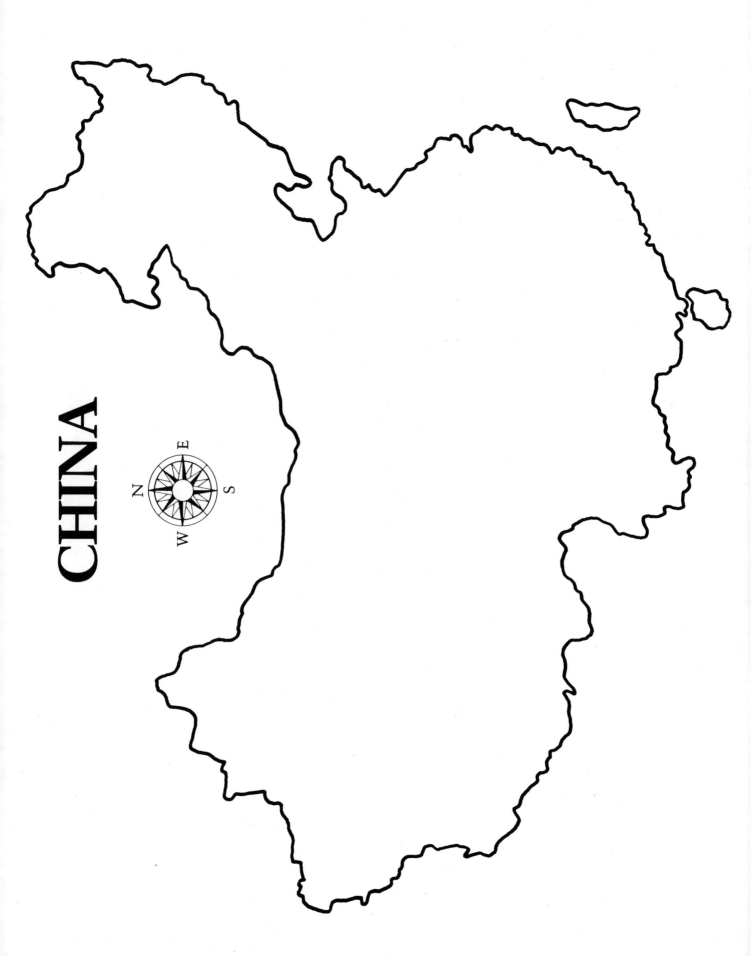

LESSON 2

American Images of China: PART 2

QUESTIONNAIRE FOLLOW-UP

Tabulate the students' answers, return and discuss the questionnaire from Lesson 1. Make note of any statistical patterns in the answers to specific questions.

AMERICAN IMAGES OF CHINA

Discuss with students their images of China. Although they are too young to have lived through even the most recent of the periods discussed in this lesson, they may have absorbed some of their images of China from sources such as old films, comic books, or stories heard from adults. Ask them to recall films of China, old or recent. Compare their images of other countries: Vietnam, Japan, or the Soviet Union.

According to Harold Isaacs,* American images of China have gone through cycles, swinging from uncritical admiration in the earliest years of discovery of China's rich civilization and culture, to contempt during the years of China's weakness and decline. Compare this pattern with our perceptions of Japan, beginning with its invasion of Manchuria in 1931, down to the present image of *Japan as Number One* (title of book by Ezra Vogel). Here is Harold Isaacs' typology of American images of China in different periods:

The Age of Respect	Eighteenth Century
The Age of Contempt	1840–1905
The Age of Benevolence	1905–1937
The Age of Admiration	1937–1944
The Age of Disenchantment	1944–1949
The Age of Hostility	1949–1972
[Age of Restored Friendship]	1972–[added by author]

During each of these periods, Americans viewed China in a special way. During the *Age of Respect* (eighteenth century), America was still a rough, frontier nation, while China was known for its elegant products, such as silks, lacquerware, cloisonné, and delicate chinaware.

*From *Scratches on Our Minds: American Images of China and India*, John Day, 1958.

In the final decades of the Qing (Ching) Dynasty in the *Age of Contempt* (1840–1905), China appeared hopelessly backward and corrupt. The Chinese seemed incapable of resisting the impact of the Western powers pushing into China with industrial goods, modern gunboats, and a bewildering array of new ideas.

After the overthrow of the Manchus in 1911, China went through decades of internal unrest, fragmentation and disunity, without an effective central government. The period was marked by famines, civil war, and great suffering. Americans contributed generously to missionary hospitals, schools, and famine relief programs such as United China Relief during this *Age of Benevolence* (1905–1937).

OUTLINE HISTORY OF U.S.–CHINA RELATIONS

1715–1842	Tea trade, clipper ships, no foreigners allowed in China.
1754	First American ship arrives in Canton.
1840–1842	Opium War between Britain and China.
1844	Treaty of Wanghia, U.S. participates in benefits of the "unequal treaties"; missionaries, traders and diplomats allowed into five treaty ports.
1865	End of second Opium War; expanded unequal treaties open China's interior and more ports to Americans and other foreigners.
1899	"Open Door Policy" promulgated by U.S. Secretary of State, John Hay, giving U.S. equal benefits in China with other nations.
1900	Boxer Uprising suppressed by foreign armies, including Americans. Americans establish fund for education with Boxer indemnity money.
1911–1937	Manchu Dynasty falls; Republican period, warlords, Chiang Kai-shek comes to power; Japanese attack China in 1937.
1937–1945	Sino-Japanese War, U.S. sympathizes with China, provides military aid following Pearl Harbor.
1945–1949	U.S. Marshall Mission fails to halt the civil war. U.S. provides economic and military aid to the Nationalist government until its defeat and expulsion in 1949.
1949–1972	U.S. cuts off all relations with the Communist government of China, gives its support to the refugee government on Taiwan. 1972, President Nixon visits China, signs the Shanghai Communiqué.
1979	U.S. and China establish normal diplomatic, cultural and trade relations.

After Japan's brutal attack and invasion of China in 1937, American news media portrayed China's suffering and heroic resistance through eight long years. After Pearl Harbor, China and the Chinese people became allies in the war against Japan.

The *Age of Admiration* (1937–1944) ended about 1944, as American GIs and journalists in China during the final years of the war reported corruption, misgovernment, and exploitation of a suffering people. This began the *Age of Disenchantment* (1944–1949), which climaxed with the downfall of Chiang Kai-shek and the Communist victory in 1949.

The *Age of Hostility* (1949–1972) and mutual isolation of our two countries ended in 1972 with President Nixon's unprecedented visit to Peking. The Korean and Vietnam wars, and the anti-Communist purges of the McCarthy period (early 1950s), had influenced American attitudes about China for two decades. The *Age of Restored Friendship* (1972–Present), began with President Nixon's trip to China, and the signing of the Shanghai Communiqué in 1972.

With the end of the Vietnam War, the threat of Communist expansion (the so-called "domino theory") in Southeast Asia subsided. Trade and cultural exchanges with China expanded year by year. China was seen more as an ally against the Soviet threat than as a danger to American interests in Asia. Americans and Chinese once again looked on one another as friends. By 1983, more than 12,000 Chinese students and scholars were studying in American universities, and nearly 200,000 Americans visited China in that year.

LESSON REVIEW

QUESTIONS FOR DISCUSSION

1. Discuss how images of another nation or its people can be formed by false perceptions, inaccurate information, by emotions triggered by events such as wars and revolutions, and by distortions of historical reality. Also note the role played by the news media in forming these images. U.S. involvement in the Vietnam War is a specific example. The "domino theory"—the fear of one billion nuclear-armed Chinese steam-rolling through southeast Asia—was cited by Secretary of State Dean Rusk as a primary reason for U.S. engagement in the war. In fact, Chinese troops never fought in that war.

2. Ask the students to call up images of other nations and peoples, how these images were formed, and how they have changed Germany, Japan, Mexico, Cuba, and Africa.

3. Discuss the reasons why the United States waited so long before initiating contacts with the People's Republic of China leading to normalization of relations. Discuss the McCarthy period, the Korean and the Vietnam wars, our ties with Taiwan, and U.S. hostility with the Soviet Union. Ask the students to suggest reasons why President Nixon decided it would be good for American interests to normalize relationships with China.

STUDENT INTERVIEWS

Ask the students to share their experiences in conducting interviews with adults, both orally and in written form. Summarize and comment on the results.

CLASS ASSIGNMENT

Read the history of the Opium War (1839–1842) and the Boxer Uprising (1899), from a textbook, encyclopedia or recommended bibliography.

LESSON 3

Religion in China: An Introduction

PURPOSE

The purpose of this series of seven lessons on religion in China is two-fold. First, the students will learn something of the basic teachings of China's traditional religions, the introduction of Christianity, and how the religions have fared in modern times. Second, the discussion questions and class activities are designed to stimulate the students to reflect on the reasons for religious belief, and how they correspond to fundamental questions about meaning and purpose in their own lives.

The seven lessons are as follows:

INTRODUCTION TO RELIGION IN CHINA

Many Americans do not know that religious beliefs and practice have survived under a Marxist government in China. In fact, after a dark period of repression, there is strong evidence of a revival of religious practice all over China. This includes Christians, Buddhists, Moslems, and, to a lesser extent, Daoists and participants in local folk religions.

Although there have been periods of repression and persecution since the inauguration of the Communist government in 1949, the official position has been one of toleration, resulting from the Marxist belief that religion will wither away as the people become educated in "scientific materialism." Since 1979, the government has restored the policy of freedom of religious belief contained in Article 36 of the Chinese Constitution. Churches, mosques, and temples by the thousands have re-opened, holy scriptures are being published, and theological seminaries are once again training Buddhist, Christian, and Moslem clergy.

Does this mean that the Chinese leaders do not follow the Marxist views of religion? By no means: China's attitude toward religion is rigidly Marxist, believing that religion originated among primitive tribes and peoples who created their own supernatural explanations for the mysteries of nature, creation, and the universe in the pre-scientific age. Later, religion was used by the power elite, they say, to oppress and delude the exploited classes, using religion as the "opiate of the people" to promise happiness in life hereafter, rather than here on earth.

In the words of Mao Zedong (1938):

> *The history of science furnishes man with proof of the material nature of the world and of the fact that it is governed by [scientific] laws, and helps man to see the futility of the illusions of religion and idealism and to arrive at materialist conclusions.*

Why would a Marxist government allow religion to flourish, when the official view of religion follows the Marxist line? The present leaders are quite candid, saying they need the cooperation of all citizens of China, including religious believers, to build a strong, unified and modernized China. Because China has a common border with the Soviet Union over 4,000 miles in length, and many non-Chinese tribes and ethnic minorities inhabit the border provinces, the national government tolerates and encourages the religions and customs of the minority groups in order to ensure their loyalty.

DAOISM, ISLAM, AND BUDDHISM

Among the four recognized religions in China today (Buddhism, Daoism, Islam, and Christianity), only Daoism (Taoism) originated in China. Tradition says that Lao-tzu ("The Old Master") was the founder. Although Dao means "the Way," Daoism has never developed a standard set of teachings. The best-known writing is the *I Ching*, popular among Western seekers after Eastern religious truth. But the symbolism of the *I Ching* is obscure, and Daoism through the centuries has evolved into an uncoordinated miscellany of beliefs and practices, including alchemy, magic, and the search for an elixir of immortality. One of the best-known but enigmatic Daoist sayings is attributed to Chuang-tzu, who said he had dreamed that he was a butterfly playing in the sunshine and after he awoke he was not sure whether he was Chuang-tzu who had dreamed that he was a butterfly, or a butterfly dreaming that it was Chuang-tzu. Popular Daoism degenerated into magic and shamanistic practices, and today is often regarded more as a legacy of folk superstitions than as an organized religion.

Moslems are the most numerous among the religious believers of the border provinces, with Lamaistic Buddhists next. Islam came to China in the eighth and ninth centuries, brought from the Middle East and Central Asia by traders, seamen and adventurers across land and sea routes. Chinese Moslems worship in thousands of mosques, concentrated largely in the northern and northwestern provinces. Moslems in

China practice their religion in the same way as Moslems elsewhere, reading from the Koran, praying five times daily, worshipping on the Sabbath, and honoring the annual religious festivals, including the month of Ramadan. In recent years Chinese Moslem delegations have made the pilgrimage to Mecca. There are an estimated fifteen million Moslems in China.

Buddhism came to China from India, the land of its origin and the home of its founder, Gautama Buddha, born about 500 B.C. Monks, pilgrims, and travelers brought the holy scriptures to China where they were translated and, through the years, spread throughout the nation beginning in the first century A.D.

Through the centuries, millions of Chinese adopted Buddhism as their religious faith, evidently finding spiritual nourishment that was not available from the humanism of Confucianism, or the magic rituals and beliefs of Daoism. Mahayana Buddhism became the Chinese version of the original Indian Buddhism, adapting to the Chinese culture and mind-set, and incorporating aspects of Confucianism.

Virtually all Chinese families formerly practiced some Buddhist customs and rituals, particularly at weddings, funerals and certain religious days during the year. Yet Buddhism as a force in Chinese life and thought has diminished in the past century, and has fallen victim to the influences of modernism, civil disorder, the erosion of traditional culture, and government policies calling for secularization of monks and nuns.

POPULAR RELIGION IN THE VILLAGES

There is no single major religion in China, as in Western and Islamic countries. Families traditionally observed Buddhist, Confucian, and Daoist rituals throughout the year. The Chinese did not become members, joining a single religious group. Religion was centered more in the home and neighborhood than in a religious building or institution.

However, there were temples and shrines to many deities. The temples in China, Taiwan, and elsewhere contain a panoply of gods representing a full range of personal and social needs. The function of the largest number was to undergird the well-being of the family and clan, the village, district, and nation. Others were devoted to the general moral order, with deities of both heaven and the underworld. Still others were patrons of crafts, trade, commerce, and agriculture, while the most-frequented temples were those to protect health and personal welfare. A single temple often contained Buddhist, Daoist, and other images and religious symbols.

In a study of Ding County in northern China, the average of seven temples per village in 1883 declined to 1.9 per village in 1928. Even so, there was still one temple for each 500 families in the latter year. Studies in other parts of China at that time showed comparable figures. While no statistics on the current situation are available, visitors to China seldom find village temples and shrines today; villagers have said that they were torn down, or converted to schools, warehouses, shops, or other uses. Even the graves were leveled or moved to make way for crops or buildings. Recent news stories from China report that new temples and shrines are being built, particularly in the villages.

It is often said that the Chinese are this-worldly and practical, in contrast to other peoples. Confucianism has a strong, secular view of life that people are basically good, and it seeks to improve the conduct of persons and the orderliness of society and government. Buddhism, on the other hand, takes a pessimistic view of life on earth and seeks escape from the pain and sorrow of life into a state of non-being called Nirvana.

LESSON REVIEW

A CLASSROOM EXERCISE: What Is Life All About?

This exercise may be used to begin this lesson. (It has been found very effective in field-testing.) Ask the students to reflect on, write about, and then to discuss these basic questions about the meaning and purpose of life. Both students and parents have commented on this activity, saying it made a greater impact than anything else in the entire series of lessons. (Note: Students do respond to what are essentially religious questions, even though they may declare themselves to be non-believers.)

Ask the students to answer briefly each of the following questions on "What is life all about." As they hand in their papers (unsigned), shuffle the papers, scanning their answers. When all the papers are in, begin reading selected questions and answers. The discussion will move on its own momentum from there.

1. What is your goal in life?

2. What do you fear most?

3. What do you think is the greatest cause of personal unhappiness in human lives in any society?

4. What do you think happens to a person after death?

5. What are your reasons for wanting to go on living?

GUIDELINES FOR DISCUSSION

The discussion following the written exercise does not have to follow religious guidelines or terminology. Rather, let students talk freely about these questions, taking the discussion wherever it may go. Some will see the religious nature of these questions; others will reject it. In any case, the discussion of these questions about the meaning of life makes a natural springboard for a study of Chinese religions and Christianity, and the search for meaning and purpose in China today, as exemplified by the letters to the editor of *Chinese Youth* magazine, "What Is the Meaning of Life?" (see Lesson 13: "What Is the Meaning of Life?").

CLASS ASSIGNMENT

Read the life of Buddha and the story of the growth of Buddhism in India. Or, read about Buddhism in China, Japan or Korea.

W·O·R·K·S·H·E·E·T

VOCABULARY REVIEW FOR LESSON 3
Religion in China: An Introduction

Name _____ Period _____ Date _____

Define the following terms:

toleration _____
_____

seminary _____
_____

supernatural _____
_____

Nirvana _____
_____

deity _____
_____

illusions _____
_____

ethnic minorities _____
_____

Islam, Moslem _____
_____

Mosque _____
_____

Koran _____
_____

shamanistic _____
_____

Mecca _____
_____

Sabbath _____
_____

secular _____
_____

opiate _____
_____

LESSON 4

Buddhism

The purpose of this lesson is to introduce the teachings of Buddhism, to evoke discussion on how Buddhism deals with the basic questions on the meaning and purpose of life raised in the previous class session, and to compare and contrast Buddhism with the Judeo-Christian view of life.

BASIC BUDDHIST BELIEFS

Buddhism originated in India in the sixth century B.C., and was brought to China by pilgrim monks in the first and second centuries A.D. For Gautama Buddha, the founder, the goal of life was to escape from the suffering and evil that afflict all people. How can we escape from this inexorable fate? *Nirvana*—the final escape from the endless succession of births and rebirths—is the ultimate goal. Nirvana means cessation, as snuffing-out a candle puts an end to light and heat, but it does not necessarily mean death. It simply means the annihilation of the fatal three-fold fire of Passion, Wrath, and Ignorance. It means the annihilation of all that binds humans to earthly life—the delusions of life which veil us from the glory of the light beyond.

In Buddhist tradition there can be visible Nirvana, achieved by an *arhat*, or saint, who continues to live a selfless life on earth; and invisible, absolute Nirvana, meaning the state following death. Nirvana, in our earthly state, is the condition in which the passions of the body no longer strive against the spirit, and the spirit attains a joy unknown to ordinary mortals.

Salvation for the Buddhist is the achievement of Nirvana, and it is achieved by self-discipline. Since life and suffering are inseparable, and the origin of suffering is desire and greed, then the elimination of desire will result in escape from suffering and the achievement of Nirvana.

THE FOUR BASIC TRUTHS, AND THE EIGHT-FOLD PATH

The Buddhist must recognize the *Four Basic Truths* and follow the *Eight-Fold Path*. For one who truly follows this discipline, Nirvana is possible. When Gautama, the founder, achieved Enlightenment, he had been freed from the evils which drag down the lives of all humans. Nirvana meant freedom, inward peace, joy, the end of all human desires and disappointment. He had reached a state in which birth, age, sickness, defilement, desire, pain and death had ceased.

The *Four Basic Truths* are:

1. Suffering is a part of every human life.

2. The cause of suffering is greed, desire, the thirst for pleasure and wealth, and the clinging to existence.

3. The way to escape this life of suffering is to get rid of desire and greed.

4. To be freed from this life of suffering, one must follow the eight-fold path, thereby breaking the endless chain of rebirth. (Explain to students the belief in reincarnation/transmigration.)

The *Eight-Fold Path* includes:

1. The first step on the Eight-Fold Path is *right views and beliefs.* By this Buddha meant a knowledge of the four basic truths and related beliefs.

2. The second step is *right aspirations,* or right resolves, meaning renunciation of pleasures, abstaining from malice and from all violence.

3. The third step is *right speech,* meaning abstention from deceit, slander, lies, and from harsh words, bad language, and foolish chatter.

4. The fourth step is *right conduct.* The follower must not kill, steal, or be guilty of immorality. Because of this teaching, Buddhists are vegetarians and advocates of non-violence, abstaining from eating meat or anything requiring the taking of life.

5. The fifth step is the *right means of livelihood.* This means withdrawing from work that brings harm to living things, such as that of the butcher, the slave dealer, the prostitute, the weapons maker, the seller of poison, and the tax collector.

6. The sixth step is *right effort,* meaning self-discipline to overcome wrong thoughts and wrong states of mind, such as resentment, sloth, and hatred.

7. The seventh step is *right mindedness.* One must be master of one's body and mind, getting rid of covetousness, selfishness, and all bad habits. "All we are is the result of what we have thought."

8. The final step in the Eight-Fold Path is *right concentration and meditation*, bringing inner peace, a full understanding of the four noble truths, and a clarity of insight called Enlightenment—"the final elimination of delusion, craving and hostility."

The Five Commandments of Buddhism are:

1. Do not kill.
2. Do not steal.
3. Do not lie.
4. Do not be unchaste.
5. Do not drink intoxicants.

To some people, while Buddhism appears to be self-centered in its search for salvation or liberation from this world, to others the teaching of Buddha inspires exemplary lives and human virtues such as compassion, selflessness, equanimity, non-violence, courage, and spiritual wisdom. There are those who think that of all the great religions the moral values of Buddhism and Christianity are the most similar. Buddhist art has inspired people of many cultures to lofty ideas, contemplation, and compassionate service to others.

CHINESE BUDDHISM

Buddhism came to China from India in the first century A.D., brought by traders from Central Asia, and by Chinese pilgrims who went to India to bring back the sacred scriptures for translation into Chinese. Buddhism in later centuries, although imported from a foreign country, came to be seen as one of the Three Teachings or Three Religions of China, along with Daoism and Confucianism.

If the Chinese are basically this-worldly and very practical in their attitudes toward life, then how could Buddhism, which takes a pessimistic view of life, find a response in China? The answer is two-fold. Buddhism provided an answer to those who indeed had suffered in life. But instead of offering Nirvana, or extinction of everything this-worldly, Buddhist beliefs were changed in China, offering two forms of salvation, or eternal life. One form of immortality was to live in Paradise—called Pure Land or Western Paradise—forever. The other was to achieve eternal Buddhahood, or sainthood. Buddhahood was understood as a higher form of life, beyond human life on earth.

These Buddhas, or bodhisattvas, were people who had lived good lives on earth, and whose merit and compassion helped other people to achieve salvation. It was these bodhisattvas who in later centuries were revered as gods in Chinese temples, their carved images worshipped in thousands of Chinese temples. In these ways, Chinese Buddhism was drastically changed from Indian Buddhism. No longer pessimistic, it offered hope and eternal life; no longer non-theistic, it offered gods to be worshipped. In these ways Buddhism appealed to many people, where Confucianism had failed.

LESSON REVIEW

QUESTIONS FOR DISCUSSION

1. What is the Buddhist view of human life? Compare that with the view of Thomas Jefferson who wrote in the Declaration of Independence:

   We hold these truths to be self-evident—that all men are created equal; that they are endowed by their Creator with certain unalienable rights; that among these are life, liberty, and the pursuit of happiness.

   (Buddha made no mention of God, either as Creator or as source of salvation. For him the only way to salvation was by personal self-discipline; the pursuit of the material things and pleasures of life on earth were not worth the struggle, pain and suffering.)

2. Compare the Buddhist goal in life with the typical life goals of American young people.

3. Compare the Buddhist teaching on the causes of unhappiness in life on earth with those given by your students in the class exercise "What Is Life All About?"

4. Compare the answers given by your students to the question, "What do you think happens to a person after death?" with the Buddhist concept of Nirvana.

5. Discuss your students' reasons for wanting to go on living, in contrast to the Buddhists' emphasis on deliverance from this life on earth.

CLASS ASSIGNMENT

Look up the Ten Commandments in the Bible *(Deuteronomy 5:6–21)* or the teachings of Jesus in the Sermon on the Mount *(Matthew 5:21–48)*. Compare these Judeo-Christian teachings on "the way of life" with the teachings in the Buddhist Eight-Fold Path, the Four Basic Truths, and the Five Commandments of Buddhism. Compare them with regard to attitudes toward life on earth, relations between persons, and the central focus of these teachings.

W·O·R·K·S·H·E·E·T

VOCABULARY REVIEW FOR LESSON 4
Buddhism

Name _____ Period _____ Date _____

Define the following terms:

Nirvana _____

_____

reincarnation, rebirth _____

_____

Four Basic Truths _____

_____

Eight-Fold Path _____

_____

aspiration _____

_____

contemplation _____

_____

meditation _____

_____

compassionate _____

_____

livelihood _____

_____

sloth _____

_____

covetousness _____

_____

delusion _____

_____

annihilation _____

_____

immorality _____

_____

intoxicant _____

_____

LESSON 5

Confucius and His Teachings

LESSON PURPOSE

The purpose of the next two lessons is (**1**) to introduce students to Confucius and the Confucian influence on Chinese society, culture, and values down to the twentieth century, and (**2**) to provoke discussion on the strengths and weaknesses of the Confucian way of life for persons of today's world.

LESSON STRATEGIES

Summarize the life of Confucius, the confused political and social situation during his lifetime, his yearning for social and political stability, and some of his central teachings. Refer to works by C. K. Yang, Huston Smith, John K. Fairbank, Lucien Pye, and D. Howard Smith in the Guide to Resources section at the end of this book for additional information.

Present the impact of Confucianism on Chinese life and culture through subsequent centuries. The teachings of Confucius were designed to promote a stable government by teaching virtues and harmonious relationships. The result was a static, conservative society, frozen in traditional forms and values, ruled by a rigid bureaucratic elite, and unable to meet the challenges of the dynamic West.

The "five relationships" established a hierarchical society in which each person knew his or her role: between ruler and subject, neighbor and neighbor, father and son, husband and wife, and brother and brother. Age and social status always had precedence, as did men over women.

Five of Confucius's central concepts stressed the importance of correct behavior. Those were *ren* (benevolence), *li* (ritual), *de* (virtue), *yi* (righteousness), and *xiao* (filial piety). Explain how these Confucian values correlate with Judeo-Christian values.

Confucius and his followers taught the "Doctrine of the Mean" (the middle way), harmony, and correct social relationships. Their respect for their elders, and for the ancestors, placed great importance on the family, and particularly on the male elders. Note the importance of having a son to carry on the family name. Chinese society became male-dominated, conservative, and placed great emphasis on tradition, harmony (don't rock the boat), and on "face."

Describe how Confucianism provided stability to Chinese government and society on the one hand, while that very quality of conservatism became the main obstacle for modernization, leaving China unprepared for the onslaught of foreign power and influence in the nineteenth and twentieth centuries.

THE ANTI-CONFUCIAN CAMPAIGN IN MODERN CHINA

Confucianism was derided by the younger, educated generation in the early twentieth century. They said that the Confucian political and social system was anti-democratic, conservative, and unable to meet the challenges of the modern world. Confucius, they said, gave special status to the scholar class. Moreover, women were subject to men in the social ladder that typified old China.

During the Communist period, there have been repeated campaigns against Confucius and his teachings. Excerpts of anti-Confucius criticism, published by young Red Guards in the 1960s, appear on page 89 of the Primary Source section at the back of the book. Discuss the reasons why the Red Guards would speak this way about Confucius and his teachings. Note that since the death of Mao there has been a partial rehabilitation of Confucius.

LESSON REVIEW

CLASS ACTIVITIES: Role Playing

1. Role play the Confucian "five relationships" (for younger students), show-ing the subservience of women, the precedence of older persons and those with higher status. This can be acted out with two persons going through a doorway. Chinese will always defer to the other before going through a door, but the older person, the man, or the one with higher status will end up going through first. Or, children can kow-tow to their father (or a citizen to the emperor), kneeling and touching the forehead three times to the floor.

2. Ask several of the students to role play the dialogue between Red Guards and the Confucian scholars. Read the "The Confucian Debate" on page 89, having each student take a part. Following the reading, open the class to spontaneous dialogue on the issues raised.

CLASS ASSIGNMENT

Read about the life and teachings of Confucius in encyclopedias or text-books. What are the most important differences between Buddhism and Confucianism?

W·O·R·K·S·H·E·E·T

VOCABULARY REVIEW FOR LESSON 5

Confucius and His Teachings

Name _____ Period _____ Date _____

Define the following terms:

hierarchical _____

_____

benevolence _____

_____

ritual _____

_____

virtue _____

_____

righteousness _____

_____

Doctrine of the Mean _____

_____

harmony _____

_____

"face" _____

_____

subservience _____

_____

precedence _____

_____

reactionary _____

_____

propriety _____

_____

criteria _____

_____

exploiter _____

_____

LESSON 6

Is Confucianism a Religion?

CONFUCIANISM— A WAY OF LIFE

The teachings of Confucius, in contrast to those of Buddha, set forth a way of life for this world—not a means to escape from it. Confucius was a humanist, and an optimist about human life. He believed that by following patterns of moral behavior, the individual, the family, and the nation would thrive.

Confucius said:

> *If there be righteousness in the heart, there will be beauty in the character.*
>
> *If there be beauty in the character, there will be harmony in the home.*
>
> *If there be harmony in the home, there will be order in the nation.*
>
> *If there is harmony in the nation, there will be peace in the world.*[1]

For Confucius, to maintain correct human relationships was all-important. These relationships involve both dependence and responsibilities. To be human is to fulfill these relationships. To abandon one's family and other obligations and become a wandering monk, is unthinkable. To this day, the family is the foundation block of Chinese society, and ritual respect for the ancestors is still practiced in many Chinese homes. Children are expected to follow careers that benefit the whole family, and arranged marriages are still common in the countryside.

Confucianism is not a religion in the conventional sense. Confucius was not a theist. While he did not worship or acknowledge a God, neither did he rule out a transcendent power. He spoke of *tien* (heaven), and accepted the existence of a spirit world. Confucius taught a *way of life* by which the individual, the family, and all people in the nation

1. *The Analects*, XVII:9

29

could live together in harmony. He did not establish a mode of worship, or a religious belief system. He never intended his teachings to be accepted as God-given ultimate truths (like the Bible or Koran), but only as human wisdom.

When Fan Ch'ih, a disciple, asked about wisdom, Confucius said:

> *Devote yourself earnestly to the duties due to men, and respect spiritual beings but keep them at a distance. This may be called wisdom.*[2]

"If we are not yet able to serve man, how can we serve spiritual beings?" Tsu-lu asked and then said, "I venture to ask about death." Confucius said:

> *If we do not yet know about life, how can we know about death?*[3]

WHAT DID CONFUCIUS SAY?

The teachings of Confucius are short sayings recorded by his students and handed down in a small volume, *The Analects of Confucius.* Confucius was a minor official, who lived in a time of warring kingdoms and civil unrest, in the state of Lu of northeastern China, in the middle of the sixth century B.C. He was a victim of the disorder of his times, and devoted himself to seeking ways to bring order into individual lives, into society, and the nation.

When he lost his political office, he spent the remainder of his years wandering from state to state attempting to find a feudal ruler who would put his ideas into action. Being an educated man, he acquired students who became his disciples, as they recognized the profound wisdom of his teaching. The name Confucius is a transliteration of Kung Fu-zi, meaning Kung the Master, or Kung the Sage.

Confucius gave up all ambition for political fame and power. Instead, he devoted his life to the search for wisdom and truth. Power and wealth might have been his for the asking if he had compromised his beliefs, but he preferred his integrity. "With coarse food to eat, water to drink, and my bended arm for a pillow, I still have joy in the midst of these things. Riches and honors acquired by unrighteousness mean no more to me than the floating clouds."

Confucius offered various guidelines for human living in response to the questions of his students and disciples. He did not prescribe a single code of behavior, or an orthodox religious creed. Among his core teachings, two were probably more important for him than any others: these were filial piety *(xiao)* and benevolence *(ren)*. We will include examples of his teaching on both these human values for discussion.

2. *The Analects*, VI:20
3. *The Analects*, XI:11

BENEVOLENCE (*Ren*)

Ren was the supreme virtue in Confucius's view of life. The Chinese written character for *ren* consists of two parts: ⊣≡. The symbol on the left, ⊣, means "a human being," while the symbol on the right, ≡, is the number "two." *Ren* has been translated as benevolence, goodness, love, human-heartedness, and compassion. *Ren* is the particular human quality that most clearly distinguishes humans from other animals. In private life, the person of *ren* is courteous, unselfish, concerned for others, and "able to measure the feelings of others by his own." In public life, he or she is honest and diligent.

Jesus, in what is called the Golden Rule, said, "Do unto others as you would have them do unto you." Confucius, who lived 500 years before Jesus, said: "What you do not want done to yourself, do not do to others." The person of *ren* has largeness of heart that embraces all people: "Within the four seas all men are brothers." Here are some of the sayings of Confucius about the virtue, *ren:*

> *One who is not a man of human-heartedness* [ren] *cannot endure adversity for very long, nor can he enjoy prosperity for long. The man of human-heartedness is naturally at ease with humanity.*[4]

> *I have never seen one who really loves human-heartedness* [ren] *or who really hates inhumanity. One who really loves human-heartedness will not place anything above it. One who really hates inhumanity will practice human-heartedness in such a way that inhumanity will not have a chance to get at him. Is there anyone who has devoted his strength to humanity for as long as a single day? Perhaps there is such a case but I have never seen it.*[5]

> *Is human-heartedness far away? When I want it, there it is right by me.*[6]

Fan Ch'ih asked about human-heartedness. Confucius said:

> *It is to love all persons.*

He asked about knowledge. Confucius said:

> *It is to know all persons.*[7]

Tzu-zhang asked Confucius about human-heartedness. Confucius said:

> *One who can practice five things wherever he may be is a person of human-heartedness.*

4. *The Analects*, IV:2
5. *The Analects*, IV:6
6. *The Analects*, VII:29
7. *The Analects*, XII: 22

Tzu-zhang asked what the five were. Confucius said:

Earnestness, liberality, truthfulness, diligence, and generosity. If one is earnest, one will not be treated with disrespect. If one is liberal [unbiased], one will win the hearts of all. If one is truthful, one will be trusted. If one is diligent, one will be successful. And if one is generous, one will be able to enjoy the grateful response of others.[8]

8. *The Analects,* XVII:6

An eighteenth century portrayal of the Chinese philosopher Confucius (551-479 B.C.) in his library.

LESSON REVIEW

QUESTIONS FOR DISCUSSION

1. Discuss definitions of religion. Is a belief in God, or gods, necessary? Must a religion be organized, with clergy, membership rites, prescribed worship and liturgy, holy scriptures, etc.? Should religion provide guidelines for personal living that will improve life on earth like Confucianism? Or is the main purpose of religion to prepare persons for life hereafter? Why did Marx call religion the "opiate of the people"?

2. Compare the "doctrine of man" of Buddhism with that of Confucianism. Is the Buddhist view of human life on earth pessimistic, or simply realistic? Do you believe, like Confucius, that the inborn self-centeredness of human beings can be changed by ethical teaching and moral example?

3. Why do you think that Buddhism attracted so many believers in India, China, Japan, Korea, and other countries of Asia? Discuss some reasons why Buddhism does not attract most Americans. On the other hand, why does it appeal to some Americans?

4. Discuss the five qualities of human-heartedness that Confucius related to Tzu-zhang: earnestness, liberality, truthfulness, diligence, and generosity. Describe how you have seen these qualities in the life of someone you know.

5. What did Confucius mean when he said, "Is human-heartedness far away? When I want it, there it is right by me." Can you give examples of the truth of this saying from your own life?

6. Is it realistic to be a person whose life is guided by human-heartedness *(ren)*? Would people take advantage of such a person? Or would people respect and admire a person who was truly selfless, kind and generous?

7. Compare the virtues of *ren* (human-heartedness) with the teachings of another religion, such as love or charity in Christianity, social responsibility in Judaism and compassion or non-violence in Buddhism.

CLASS ASSIGNMENT

Write down your ideas on how the teachings of Confucius would be (a) suitable, and (b) unsuitable in American life today.

W·O·R·K·S·H·E·E·T

Is Confucianism a Religion?

Name _____ Period _____ Date _____

Define the following terms:

theist _____

_____

transcendent _____

_____

transliteration _____

_____

integrity _____

_____

compromise _____

_____

orthodox _____

_____

creed _____

_____

inhumanity _____

_____

humanist _____

_____

clergy _____

_____

liturgy _____

_____

doctrine of man _____

_____

ethical, moral _____

_____

earnestness _____

_____

diligence _____

_____

compassion _____

_____

LESSON 7

Filial Piety

LESSON PURPOSE

The concept of filial piety and its role in Chinese society can prompt American youth to reflect on their own relationships with parents and other elders, and the tension in American life between perceptions of individual rights and responsibilities to family and society.

Filial piety *(xiao)* means respect for one's parents and family members. It is at the heart of the Chinese family system and is the main reason that Chinese civilization has held together through an unbroken history of over 3,000 years—longer than any other nation or culture. Confucius believed that the individual learned the basic virtues of life, and built good character within the family. If one is to become an adult with human-heartedness *(ren)*, virtue *(de)*, and righteousness *(yi)*, these virtues are learned first in the home and family.

Three of the five relationships that describe an orderly society in the Confucian scheme take place in the home and family. These are relationships between father and son, elder brother and younger brother, and husband and wife; the other two are between ruler and subject, and friend to friend.

All of these relationships are reciprocal. A father should be loving, a son respectful; an elder brother gentle, a younger brother respectful; a husband good, a wife obedient; an elder friend considerate, a younger friend deferential; a ruler benevolent, a subject loyal.

There are many stories of faithful children who practiced *xiao*. In one of them a son, whose aged father was too poor to afford a mosquito net, took off his shirt to attract the mosquitoes to himself so that his father could sleep. Confucius said of this:

> *Young men should be filial when at home and respectful to their elders when away from home. They should be earnest and faithful. They should love all persons and be close to persons of human-heartedness* [ren].[1]

1. *The Analects*, I:6

35

Tzu-yu asked about filial piety. Confucius said:

> *Filial piety nowadays means to support one's parents. But we support even dogs and horses. If there is not a feeling of love and respect* [reverence], *wherein lies the difference?*[2]

The Duke of She told Confucius, "In my country there is an upright man named Kung. When his father stole a sheep, he bore witness against him in court." Confucius said: "The upright men in my community are different from this. The father conceals the misconduct of the son and the son conceals the misconduct of the father. Uprightness is to be found in this."

2. *The Analects,* II:7

LESSON REVIEW

QUESTIONS FOR DISCUSSION

1. Discuss the concept of filial piety *(xiao)* in the Chinese tradition. Compare the Confucian "five relationships," which promote a sense of person-in-community and social responsibility, with the American belief in the rights of the individual. Is there too much individualism and not enough community in the American way of life?

2. Discuss the pros and cons of the Chinese son's or daughter's primary obligation to the extended family, rather than to the self. Will this inhibit or help personal growth and maturity?

3. In the dialogue between Confucius and the Duke of She, we find two different views of what is meant by "uprightness." Compare the answer given by Confucius with the moral and legal standards we expect from men and women elected to public office in the United States. Consider why Confucius answered as he did.

4. Imagine on the one hand how the Confucian standard of prior loyalty to the family affected the efficiency of Chinese government; on the other hand, imagine a society where there is no affection or loyalty between children and parents, and where the primary loyalties are to an ideology, a political authority, or a religious cult.

5. Consider the teaching of Confucius on supporting one's parents. Discuss the increasing problem in American society of caring for the elderly, where we no longer live together in three-generation homes.

CLASS ASSIGNMENT

Write an essay describing how the main teachings of Confucius would (or would not) work well in American culture today, giving the reasons why.

W·O·R·K·S·H·E·E·T

Filial Piety

Name _____ Period _____ Date _____

Define the following terms:

virtues _____

_____

reciprocal _____

_____

misconduct _____

_____

uprightness _____

_____

filial piety _____

_____

benevolent _____

_____

deferential _____

_____

tension _____

_____

perceptions _____

_____

LESSON 8

Christianity in China

LESSON PURPOSE

The purpose of this lesson is to present a historical overview of Christianity in China, including the fate of the Christian churches under Communism, and the current revival of Christianity in the post-Mao period.

CHRISTIANITY'S BEGINNINGS IN CHINA

Christianity was brought to China from the West four different times. The first time was by the Nestorians from Asia Minor in the seventh and eighth centuries; the second, during the Mongol (Yuan) Dynasty of the thirteenth and fourteenth centuries. This was the time of Marco Polo's China adventures. Franciscan missionaries, fellow-Italians of Marco Polo, brought Christianity to China at that time. No one knows the fate of thousands of Christians who simply disappeared from history when the Chinese dynasties changed from Tang to Sung (960), and Yuan to Ming (1368). There are no surviving historical records.

JESUIT MISSIONARIES AND THE RITES CONTROVERSY

The third Christian venture had more lasting success. Catholic missionaries, this time Jesuits from Europe, established Christianity first in the capital city, Peking, and from there throughout the provinces. The most famous of these was Matteo Ricci, a well-educated scholar who was respected in China for his knowledge of modern science, mathematics, and astronomy. The four-hundredth anniversary of Ricci's arrival in China was celebrated in 1983. Ricci and his colleagues became skilled in the Chinese language, wrote books in Chinese about Christianity, dressed in Chinese robes, and were respected by Chinese scholars, officials, and the Imperial Court.

The Jesuit missionaries made efforts to adapt Christianity to Chinese culture and customs. The most controversial was their belief that the ancestral rites practiced by every Chinese family were not religious ceremonies, but were merely a means of showing respect. After years of controversy, Pope Clement XII issued a decree in 1715 forbidding the practice of ancestral rites in Christian homes or services.

Angered at this interference in the internal affairs of China by an outside power, the Chinese emperor ordered the expulsion of the missionaries. This began a period of persecution of Christians, thus ending nearly 150 years of Christian growth. At the time, there were an estimated 300,000 Christians located in several provinces throughout China.

Father Matteo Ricci—Jesuit missionary.

CHRISTIANITY IN MODERN TIMES

The fourth time Christianity from the West entered China was after the Opium War (1839–1842), when China was forced to open up its ports to foreign merchants, diplomats, and missionaries. For many years prior to that date, foreigners had been forbidden to set foot in China, except for a small island used for trading in Canton harbor. Westerners were protected from Chinese law by the "unequal treaties," which provided that foreigners guilty of a crime in China could not be arrested and tried in Chinese courts. American and European gunboats patrolled Chinese rivers and coastlines. This provision of the treaties, called *extraterrito-*

riality, was not revoked by the Western nations until 1943. Naturally, this was resented by all patriotic Chinese. Since missionaries were also protected, there was considerable anti-Christian sentiment and, in some cases, demonstrations and riots. The century following the first Opium War is often called the "century of humiliation." The Boxer Uprising, in which 242 foreigners and many Chinese Christians were killed, was the worst of the anti-foreign incidents.

Protestant missionaries entered China for the first time in the 1840s. At the same time, Catholic missionaries renewed their efforts, which had dwindled to almost nothing. By 1900, there were 3800 Protestant and Catholic missionaries, and 800,000 Chinese Christians—one-seventh Protestant, and the remainder Catholic. By 1949, there were about 700,000 Protestants and over three million Catholics, with parishes in every province of China. Protestants were concentrated in the cities and coastal provinces, while Catholics worked mainly in the villages and rural areas.

Missionaries brought more than religious doctrine into China. They came at a time when rapid population growth and breakdown of effective government had brought disruption, civil unrest, banditry, and hardship. Famines, plagues, and epidemic disease caused widespread suffering. Missionaries opened thousands of schools, hospitals, local clinics, homes for lepers, feeding stations during famines, orphanages, and rural development projects. For the first time, girls had access to public schooling. Nursing schools were opened. Over half the hospitals in China in the 1930s were mission-sponsored. Missionaries also campaigned against foot-binding, helping to end this painful, demeaning, and crippling custom to women.

While four million Christians in 1949 was a significant number—making an impact all over China with their educational, medical and other social service projects—they still numbered less than one percent of the total population of 500 million at that time. Following the Communist victory in 1949, missionaries began to leave. By 1952, almost all of them were gone, except for a few held in prison or under house arrest.

THE CHURCH UNDER COMMUNISM

Since 1949, the Protestant and Catholic Christians have gone through cycles of toleration and repression, but have emerged in recent years as lively and growing communities. They emphasize their selfhood as a Chinese church, without missionaries or foreign financial support. The schools, hospitals, and other projects have been nationalized, but Christians are allowed to worship in their parish churches. Chinese pastors and priests, most of them in their sixties, seventies, or older, provide ministerial services. Over one million copies of the Bible, in Chinese, have been printed since 1980, and nearly a dozen seminaries for training clergy (Catholic and Protestant) have reopened.

Since 1979, nearly two thousand parish churches have been repaired and reopened. Foreign visitors have reported Sunday services packed with worshippers, many of them young people. Chinese church leaders say that more people are attending church now than in 1949. In the rural areas, where there are no clergy or churches, many are meeting in private homes. According to recent estimates (1984), there are at least six million Christians in China today, with some estimates running much higher.

Religion is confined to churches and temples. There is no religious broadcasting, advertising, or publishing of books and magazines outside the churches. Religion is not allowed in the schools, except for negative views of religion based on the teachings of Marx and Engels. The teaching and practice of religion is confined to churches, temples, mosques, and the homes of believers.

One reason that Christians kept their faith alive during years of suppression was what the Chinese call "house meetings." Christians all over China would gather in small groups in their homes for prayer and Bible study. When their pastors and priests were sent to prisons or labor camps, these house meetings were led by the lay people of the churches. Many new Christians were added during these years.

There are many moving stories of these small "house meetings." Raymond Fung, a Hong Kong Christian, collected some of these by interviewing Chinese Christians, and they were published in a small book called *Households of God on China's Soil*. An excerpt from one of these stories is included in the Primary Sources, on page 92.

LESSON REVIEW

QUESTIONS FOR DISCUSSION

1. Discuss some reasons for, or against, sending Christian missionaries to another country. Why is the situation different for missionaries in a country like China compared to one of the Latin American countries?

2. Discuss and reflect on the impact of religion in America. Consider the loss to our society and culture if a hostile government in Washington should force all religious expression to cease, including schools, colleges, hospitals, nursing homes, day-care centers, inner-city projects, works of charity, art, music, films, drama, publications, and places of worship.

3. How can a missionary be of service in another country without imposing his or her own culture? Discuss the meaning of the term "cultural imperialism" as applied to missionaries and their work.

4. Why does Christianity survive in China under Communism, and why is it tolerated?

5. Copy and distribute the excerpt from "A Christian Village," found in Primary Sources on page 92. Discuss this example of a "house church" and compare it with a typical American church or synagogue.

6. What do you think about the future of the Church in China?

CLASS ASSIGNMENT

1. How did Mao's early years and experience prepare him to be a revolutionary leader?

2. Read about the Boxer Rebellion (1900). Pretend you are a patriotic Chinese at that time, and explain why the Boxers rose up against the foreigners.

W·O·R·K·S·H·E·E·T

VOCABULARY REVIEW FOR LESSON 8
Christianity in China

Name _____ Period _____ Date _____

Define the following terms:

evangelism _____

_____

ancestral rites _____

_____

doctrine _____

_____

atheism _____

_____

toleration _____

_____

repression _____

_____

propagate _____

_____

cultural imperialism _____

_____

missionaries _____

_____

extraterritoriality _____

_____

revival _____

_____

persecution _____

_____

decree _____

_____

nationalized _____

_____

LESSON 9

Religion Under Communism

LESSON PURPOSE

The purpose of this lesson is to examine the Marxist/Maoist views of religion, the distinctions made between superstition and religion in China today, and the reasons why the Communists tolerate religion within strictly defined limits.

HISTORICAL BACKGROUND

Traditional religions in China were in decline long before the founding of the Chinese Communist Party in 1921. Temples and monasteries fell into disrepair during the years of civil unrest and decay of government. In Hunan Province, during the first twenty years of the Republic (1911–1931), half the temples were converted for use as public schools, while others were used as soldiers' quarters, storehouses, and public offices. The decline of religion was due in part to modern education, which brought a new generation of youth who found no answers for China's needs in the temples and ancient religions.

The Communists, believing in what they call "scientific materialism," accept the Marxist view that religion is pure illusion, with no basis in reality and with no value to the nation.

The "ultra-leftists" are now blamed for the excesses of the Cultural Revolution (1966–1979). At that time all temples, mosques, and churches were closed, and many of them were vandalized. Roving bands of Red Guards smashed Buddha figures, stained glass windows, crosses, and religious art. They believed they were destroying the "four olds"—old habits, ideas, culture, and customs.

Religious believers were forced underground, and many clergy and religious believers were put in prison or labor camps. However, religion survived in the privacy of small house groups, and the current revival of Buddhism, Islam, and Christianity in China demonstrates that religion will not quickly "wither away," as predicted by Marx. Although Communist Party members are not allowed to believe or follow any religion, neither are they allowed, under the present leaders, to persecute religion.

Freedom of religious belief is written into the new Constitution, and the new legal code.

ARTICLE 36: The Chinese Constitution (1982)

Citizens of the People's Republic of China enjoy freedom of religious belief.

No state organization, public organization or individual may compel citizens to believe in, or not to believe in, any religion; nor may they discriminate against citizens who believe in, or do not believe in, any religion.

The state protects normal religious activities. No one may make use of religion to engage in activities that disrupt public order, impair the health of citizens or interfere with the educational system of the state.

Religious bodies and religious affairs are not subject to any foreign domination.

In order to guard against a recurrence of persecution, the new legal code adopted by the Chinese government provides that any government official who deprives a citizen of the constitutional right to freedom of religious belief will be subject to up to two years of imprisonment.

MAO ZEDONG ON RELIGION

Mao Zedong, China's leader for many years until his death in 1976, was a Marxist. However, because he believed in the inevitable withering away of religion, he never publicly advocated using force or coercion to stamp it out. His 1957 remarks on religious policy have often been cited in China:

We cannot compel people to give up idealism, any more than we can force them to believe in Marxism. The only way to settle questions of an ideological nature or controversial issues among the people is by the democratic method, the method of discussion, of criticism, of persuasion and education, and not by the method of coercion or repression.

Mao's views on religion go back to his childhood and youth, long before he ever heard of Marx. While still a student, Mao linked religion with capitalism, autocracy, and Confucian class distinctions as the "four evil demons" of traditional China. Ten years later (1927), he spoke to the peasants in Hunan about liberation from the "four authorities" that had dominated them: the political, clan, religious, and male authorities.

Liberation comes from only one source, he said, the united power of the peasants. His mode of attack on religion was ridicule. Have the gods helped you to throw off your burdens, or is your new freedom due solely to your own efforts?

The gods? Worship them by all means. But if you had only Lord Kuan and the goddess of Mercy and no peasant association, could you have overthrown the local tyrants and evil gentry? The gods and goddesses are indeed miserable objects. You have worshipped them for centuries, and they have not overthrown a single one of the local tyrants or evil gentry for you! Now you want to have your rent reduced. Let me ask how will you go about it? Will you believe in the gods or in the peasant association?

During all the years prior to the Communist victory in 1949, Mao Zedong had two main goals for the Chinese Revolution, to remove the "two mountains" that burdened the backs of the Chinese people. These were foreign imperialism and Chinese feudalism.

Mao described the "four thick ropes" of feudalism which bound the Chinese people, particularly the peasants, in his *Report on an Investigation of the Peasants' Movement in Hunan* (1927). He reports on the spontaneous peasant uprisings in that province against the domination of four systems of authority: (1) the political authority from township level on up; (2) the clan authority, focused in the ancestral temple and male heads of households; (3) the religious authority, "ranging from the King of Hell down to the town and village gods"; and (4) the domination of women by men.

RELIGION AND SUPERSTITION

The Chinese government makes a clear distinction between religion and superstition. Only four main religions are protected by the Constitution; all other so-called religions or cults are considered superstitions, and are therefore illegal. The four religions are Christianity, Islam, Buddhism, and Daoism. Here are excerpts from a recent article in the Chinese press called "Do Away with Feudal Superstitions."*

> In recent years there has been a tendency for feudal superstitious activities to regain ground in our rural areas. We should pay great attention to the various feudal superstitious activities, which are harmful to our production and to the people's physical and mental health, polluting the general mood of society and affecting our unity.

> **What Are Feudal Superstitious Activities?**

> So-called feudal superstitious activities primarily denote unscientific, absurd activities, such as begging for the appearance of gods or immortals, practicing ghost writing or divination, expelling ghosts in order to cure sickness, praying for rain and for an end to natural disasters, practicing physiognomy and other fortune-telling tricks and practicing geomancy. These activities

*From *New China News Agency,* December 28, 1982.

are carried out by sorcerers, sorceresses, fortune-tellers and geomancers. They take every opportunity to spread fallacies to deceive people and defraud them of money or other property; they are harmful to our production, to social order and to the people's physical and mental health.... These activities usually combine closely with remaining feudal ideas and feudal activities to undermine the social order and poison the people's thinking.

Many of our people, particularly those in rural and pastoral areas, beg to their gods or practice divination for begetting offspring or for an end to distress or sickness, because they lack scientific knowledge and adhere to bad old habits.

Practitioners of feudal superstitions are those such as witches, sorcerers and geomancers who pretend to communicate with gods and ghosts, and those who trick people for their money by superstitious means. In the old society many of them did these things because they could not find any decent way to earn a living. Essentially, this was a disguised form of exploitation. We must adopt a policy of education and transforming them to help them turn over a new leaf, give up the parasitic life and become workers earning their own living.

The Party and State have adopted a policy of freedom of religious belief because religion is a longstanding matter, concerning millions of people.... But feudal and superstitious activities are different from this and do not belong to the realm of religion at all. Therefore the question of freedom of belief does not exist at all for feudal and superstitious activities.... Making use of religion to carry out illegal and criminal activities must be strictly forbidden. All religious believers should love the country and abide by the law.

LESSON REVIEW

QUESTIONS FOR DISCUSSION

1. The Chinese Constitution guarantees "freedom of religious belief," but it does not spell out the limits of that freedom in actual practice; nor does it protect religion from government interference (separation of church and state). Discuss the differences between Article 36 of the Chinese national Constitution and the First Amendment of the Constitution of the United States:

    Congress shall make no law respecting an establishment of religion, or prohibiting the free exercise thereof; or abridging the freedom of speech, or of the press; or the right of the people peaceably to assemble and to petition the government for a redress of grievances.

2. Would superstitious activities that are outlawed in China be permitted in the U.S.? Should so-called cult groups and witchcraft be allowed? Discuss the issue of prayer and religion in the public schools.

3. Discuss the local folk religions that Mao Zedong describes, and his reasons for ridiculing them.

4. Discuss the whole rural social system of old China (called feudalism by Mao Zedong), which gave power and wealth to a landlord-gentry class at the expense of the rural people, who made up over 80 percent of the total population.

CLASS ACTIVITY AND ASSIGNMENT

Rehearse and play-act the Chinese drama about superstition, "The Meeting of the Three Clowns," found on page 95, or continue the previous day's assignment.

W·O·R·K·S·H·E·E·T

Religion Under Communism

Name _____ Period _____ Date _____

Define the following terms:

discriminate against _____

_____

coercion _____

_____

ideological _____

_____

monastery _____

_____

divination _____

_____

sorcerer _____

_____

geomancer _____

_____

fallacy _____

_____

ultra-leftist _____

_____

idealism _____

_____

tyrant _____

_____

gentry _____

_____

illusion _____

_____

autocracy _____

_____

physiognomy _____

_____

LESSON 10

Coping with Death in China

RATIONALE FOR DEATH EDUCATION IN THE SCHOOLS

Through the writings of Elizabeth Kübler-Ross and others, Americans are facing the questions surrounding death more directly than ever before. American young people, however, are shielded from the physical facts of death. Hospitals, nursing homes, and morticians perform the final services for the terminally ill, which are conducted quite openly in the homes and neighborhoods of most Third World countries.

Yet studies have shown that death is a real concern for American children and youth. Accidents, primarily from automobiles, are the greatest cause of death among teenagers, and their suicide rate is at the highest level on record. Drug abuse, abortion, capital punishment, wars and terrorism, street crimes, mass murders, dangers from radiation and toxic waters, and the fears of nuclear megadeath lurking in their consciousness lead to a "psychic numbing" and a loss of hope for the future among many American youth today.

Educators advocate the inclusion of death education in the school curriculum. One researcher, working with randomly selected high school groups, concluded that children and youth need opportunities to discuss and reflect on the meaning of life and death.[1] There is an important relationship between an individual's orientation toward death, and his/her (1) self-concept, (2) early experiences with death, (3) psychological well-being, (4) life-style, and (5) attitude toward school.

Death education, facing directly the fundamental questions of life and death, can help young people cope with the crisis of faith and loss of meaning and purpose. In *The Denial of Death*,[2] Ernest Becker speaks of "man's tragic destiny; he must desperately justify himself as an object of primary value in the universe." Becker goes on to say that, "Whatever he does on this planet has to be done in the lived truth of the terror

---

1. R. Bennett, "Death and Curriculum" in P. Zalaznik, *Dimensions of Loss and Death Education*, Minneapolis: Edu-Pac Co., 1979, p. 3.
2. E. Becker, *The Denial of Death*, New York: Macmillan, 1973, p. 4.

of creation, of the grotesque, of the rumble of panic underneath everything.... The crisis of modern society is precisely that youth no longer feel heroic in the plan for action that their culture has set up."

> *To accept death means to take charge of one's life. The [one] who sees the genuine function of death is no fatalist. He [or she] does not feel structured. On the contrary, he [or she] is the freest of all...nothing to fear, nothing to be timid about, nothing to make him [or her] dependent, inadequate or inferior, for he [or she] has once and for all conquered the ultimate threat. The thought of death urges one to assume a total plan for...life. The vitality of death leads one to adopt an ideal or goal, a noble life, or a major achievement as the purpose of existence. Through the vitality of death, one is able to see all events in life from the perspective of...total existence.*[3]

By studying and reflecting on the experience of other peoples—in this case the Chinese—in their search for salvation, for meaning in life and the conquest of death, American young people can face these same questions in their own lives.

LESSON PURPOSE

As with other lessons in this curriculum unit, there is a dual purpose for this lesson: (1) to introduce the students to beliefs and practices pertaining to death and the afterlife in Chinese religions; and (2) to lead them into reflection and discussion of the meaning of life and death in their own lives and religious orientation.

INTRODUCTION

The basis of all religions is the search for the meaning of life and death. A current revival of religious commitment among American students and intellectuals is seen as a search for meaning and purpose beyond science and rationalism.

> *The great tragedy is not death itself, but death without meaning. The greater tragedy may be life without meaning.*[4]

Douglas Sloan, a historian at Columbia University, said recently: "The modern world view, which became dominant in science, left no room for dealing with purpose, meaning, value and left out everything that's really important."[5]

According to Daniel Bell, A Harvard social scientist:

> *The exhaustion of modernism, the aridity of Communist life, the tedium of the unrestrained self...all indicate that a long era*

---

3. R. Kastenbaum in James Kidd, *Relentless Verity: Education for Being–Becoming–Belonging,* U.S. Educational Resource Information Center, ERIC Document ED 094 158, p. 22.
4. R. Kastenbaum in James Kidd, *op. cit.,* p. 19.
5. D. Sloan, "A Return to Religion," *The New York Times Magazine,* April 15, 1984, p. 91.

is coming to a close. What people fail to realize, is that the institutions that have survived the longest are religious ones. The existential questions are always with us—love, death, tragedy, obligation. The most coherent responses...have been the religious responses.[6]

ATTITUDES TOWARD DEATH IN CHINESE RELIGIONS

Chinese religious beliefs often overlap, and "three-religion" families are commonplace in Taiwan and Southeast Asia. They observe Buddhist, Daoist, and Confucian customs throughout the year, as called for by time and occasion.

CONFUCIANISM AND DEATH

Confucius was a rationalist, a man of this world, who refused to speculate about an other-world or an after-life. He supported the cult of the ancestors because it gave stability to society. On his deathbed, when asked to pray, he said that he had been praying a long time—that is, he had lived a good life, made his contribution, and needed no special prayers to prepare for death.

Speaking about death, he said that "to know about death one must know about life." For him, to follow the Way (right living) in life was sufficient; he needed no special salvation. Confucius said:

> *If it is the will of heaven that the Way shall prevail, then the Way will prevail.*[7]

> *In the morning, hear the Way; in the evening die content.*[8]

Confucius believed that rituals *(li)* should be properly observed. Although he was not sure that a spirit-world existed, he practiced the rites *as if* the spirits existed. When Confucius offered sacrifices to his ancestors, he felt as if his ancestral spirits were actually present. When he offered sacrifices to other spiritual beings, he felt as if they were actually present. Confucius never discussed strange phenomena, physical exploits, disorder, or spiritual beings. Confucius said:

> *When parents are alive, serve them according to li, and sacrifice to them according to li.*[9]

The good Confucianist, through the centuries, has been one who observed the proper rites, customs, and social forms. As a member of the educated class, he disdained what he viewed as superstitious practices among the people—their search for enlightenment, salvation, or eternal life in the Western Paradise; their sacrifices to gods and images for special favors and protection.

6. *Ibid.*
7. *The Analects*, XIV:38.
8. *The Analects*, IV:8.
9. *The Analects*, II:5.

Enlightenment, for him, is achieved by staying in the world, and by performing social and moral duties. By practicing the right Way, one can lead a meaningful life and can face a peaceful death; there is no need to be concerned about salvation or an afterlife of the soul.

DAOISM, BUDDHISM, AND FOLK RELIGIONS: THE CONQUEST OF DEATH

For the Confucianist, the cult of the ancestors is not so much a search for personal immortality as a means to establish a stable society, a continuity of the family line, and reverence for the dead. For the ordinary people who practiced the popular religious cults—blending Buddhism, Daoism and folk religions—there was fear of the spirits and concern to service them properly. There were good spirits *(shen)* and bad spirits *(quei)*; funeral customs were designed to keep the spirits satisfied and supportive.

In contrast to the Confucian rites and teachings, the conquest of death was the goal of the popular religious beliefs and customs. Chinese Buddhism, unlike Indian Buddhism with its goal of Nirvana, emphasized personal salvation and sought ways for survival beyond this life. Salvation meant transcending death by being taken out of the endless cycle of life, to a place beyond this world—a Western Paradise, a Pure Land, or a Paradise of the Immortals.

There were two principal means of achieving salvation. One was the practice of yoga, called *Chan* in Chinese, or *Zen* in Japanese. This is the practice of meditation and self-discipline to achieve spiritual release. Piety, dedication, and withdrawal from the world are the conditions of salvation, putting one in touch with Ultimate Reality.

The second, and more popular means of salvation, was the substitution of Heaven for Nirvana. Whereas Nirvana implied the extinction of all existence, including an after-life, salvation in this second sense means achieving eternal Buddhahood, a higher form of life beyond this world. Endless variations of belief and practice evolved through the centuries, all reflected in the popular funeral customs.

MARXIST/MAOIST VIEWS OF LIFE AND DEATH

Robert Lifton, the psycho-historian, coined the term "revolutionary immortality" to describe the patriotic dedication of Chinese youth during the Cultural Revolution. To what extent does the search for this kind of secular immortality motivate Americans?

> *The revolutionary denies theology as such, but embraces a secular utopia through images closely related to the spiritual conquest of death and even to an afterlife. His revolutionary "works" are all important, and only to the extent that he can perceive them as enduring can he achieve a measure of acceptance of his own eventual death.... The overwhelming threat is not so much death itself as the suggestion that his "revolutionary works" will not endure.*[10]

In his short essay, "Serve the People," memorized by all Chinese school children in the 1960s, Mao Zedong held up as a model the duty to offer one's life, even to the point of death, in the service of the nation and the people.

> *All men must die, but death can vary in its significance. The ancient Chinese writer Szuma Chien said, "Though death befalls all men alike, it may be weightier than Mount Tai or as insignificant as a feather."... the Chinese people are suffering; it is our duty to save them.... Wherever there is struggle there is sacrifice, and death is a common occurrence. But we have the interests of the people and the sufferings of the great majority at heart, and when we die for the people, it is a worthy death.*[11]

China's leaders today are secularists, and the official ideology is based on Marxist concepts of "scientific materialism." For them, the only reality is that which can be seen, touched, scientifically tested, and made to serve the nation. Speculations about life after death are futile;

10. R. Lifton, *Revolutionary Immortality: Mao Tse-tung and the Chinese Cultural Revolution*, New York: Alfred A. Knopf, Vintage, 1968.
11. Mao Tse-tung, "Serve the People," September, 1944.

the only meaning in life comes from one's contribution here on earth. Moreover, funeral rites and customs are wasteful of money and resources, and contribute (they believe) to superstition and diversion of energies from useful work. The official policy is to eliminate these family ceremonies related to the cult of ancestors.

In a long conversation with the French writer Andre Malraux in 1965, Mao Zedong said:

> *When I said, "Chinese Marxism is the religion of the people"... I meant that the communists express the Chinese people in a real way if they remain faithful to the work upon which the whole of China has embarked as if on another Long March. When we say, "We are the Sons of the People," China understands it as she understood the phrase "Son of Heaven." The People has taken the place of the ancestors....* [12]

An American visiting China recently asked the engineer in charge of a large hydroelectric project how they had dealt with the problem of the ancestral graves long buried in the valley floor, destined to become a man-made lake when the dam was completed. About 250,000 farmers and villagers had been living there for generations. The question of the graves was a matter of political education, he explained; people had to learn that bones and graves are meaningless material remains. In most cases the graves were excavated and the bones ground up for fertilizer. For those elderly people who insisted, the graves were moved to new sites. The entire reservoir floor, an area of 580 square kilometers, was scraped clean, removing all marks and relics of its one-time human inhabitants, before it was flooded. For this civil engineer, death was a matter of logistics, not metaphysics. For him, the superstitious beliefs of the villagers could be accommodated. But the only meaningful reality was a huge dam of steel and concrete, with its backed-up reservoir and electric generating capacity.

In the campaign to increase the area of crop-land, many graves and cemeteries have been leveled in China. The practice of cremation is officially advocated, and is virtually universal now in the cities. But cremation is feared by many of the elderly, who believe the family solidarity and the ancestral succession will be disturbed; they doubt that the spirit can survive cremation. Ground burial is still permitted in the rural areas, and funerals, some of them elaborate and costly, have become commonplace following the period of repression during the Cultural Revolution. As in other matters of religious practice, traditional funeral rites and customs are tolerated by the government and party, in the belief that they will eventually disappear.

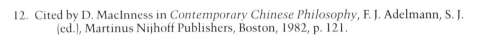

12. Cited by D. MacInness in *Contemporary Chinese Philosophy*, F. J. Adelmann, S. J. (ed.), Martinus Nijhoff Publishers, Boston, 1982, p. 121.

FILIAL PIETY AND DEATH OF THE ELDERLY

The traditional value binding Chinese society together is the centrality of the family, based on filial piety—the responsibility of children for their parents. This long-standing moral obligation is now written into Chinese law; children are required to care for their elderly parents. The three-generation family living together is the norm in China today. In the cities, pensions and social security payments support retired persons without children. In the rural areas, the "five guarantees" provide housing, food, clothing, medical care, and a decent burial. The neighborhood committee cares for the elderly living alone. At a minimum, the burial guarantee provides a wood coffin, some mourners and pallbearers, and a graveside ceremony with incense and candles.[13] More elaborate funerals are provided and paid for by filial children.

The Chinese rituals and customs surrounding old age and death, based on filial piety even today, have both pragmatic and religious values. Pragmatically, they ensure the stability and continuity of the family as the basic unit in Chinese society. Children and grandchildren learn traditional values from their elders, and in turn provide old age security for them.

The religious symbolism embodied in death rituals and customs varies from family to family, and region to region. Funeral customs among the Miao tribespeople in Yunnan Province, for example, would be far different from those among Moslems in the northwest, or Buddhists in Tibet. During the Cultural Revolution, traditional funerals of any kind were banned, and deaths were marked by simple memorial meetings. The revival of funeral customs in the rural areas is not matched in the cities, where cremation rather than burial is now the rule, and congested streets simply cannot accommodate elaborate funeral processions. Even so, a simple funeral for an elderly parent in the cities may cost the equivalent of three or four months' salary for the surviving children. Elaborate, traditional funerals in the villages can cost much more.

These are the main reasons why all Chinese adults wish to have children: to provide continuity for the family line through a son; to provide old age security for themselves; and to assure a proper funeral and burial. A fourth reason, even in China's socialized economy, is to increase the number of wage-earners in the family. This is particularly true in the rural economy today where private family farming is now encouraged, and is one reason why the national campaign for "one-child families" is not succeeding in the countryside.

13. D. Davis-Friedman, *Long Lives: Chinese Elderly and the Communist-Revolution*, Cambridge: Harvard University Press, 1983, p. 61.

CHINESE FUNERALS

The death of a family elder is the most important event in the life of a Chinese family, and requires the most elaborate and costly ceremonies. The entire extended family is involved, and periods of mourning can go on for months. In contrast, funeral ceremonies are rarely performed for a child.

Chinese funeral rites are designed to send the spirit of the departed loved one off to the other-world properly. To fail to observe correct customs might result in the endless wandering of a homeless spirit, which might bring misfortune on the family. Thus, filial duty requires proper concern for the after-life of the soul and spirit, as well as life in this world. Various religious acts assure a safe and speedy journey of the spirit to Heaven. To make the journey comfortable, the body is dressed in fine garments, and valued personal effects are placed in the coffin, while paper money, paper horses, boats, houses, furniture, and (in recent years) paper autos and airplanes are burned. Burning these objects symbolizes the transition from one life to the next, and assures the soul or spirit of a comfortable life in Heaven. The famous gravesite of the Chin Emperor in the city of Xi'an exemplifies the elaborate concern for a safe and comfortable after-life. Hundreds of life-sized, terracotta armed warriors, horses, and chariots have been unearthed in recent years, and archeologists have only begun the excavations.

While most of these religious acts were expressions of respect and affection, they also were meant to please the spirit of the dead and ward off subsequent evil influences; the living survivors sought the protection and blessing of the departed one's spirit.

Ancestral tablets were installed in the family altar or the larger ancestral hall, along with the tablets of other ancestors — sometimes over a thousand tablets in a single hall, going back thirty or forty generations. Ancestral rites and sacrifices were performed throughout the year. These included burning of incense, kowtowing to the ancestral tablets, burning candles and paper money, and the offering of food and drink (which were later consumed by the family). In the name of the ancestors, a sacrificial meal of good food symbolized the family's good fortune and abundance. Great reunion feasts brought members of the clan together around dozens, or even hundreds of tables, affirming the solidarity of the family and its unbroken continuity with past generations.

Proper observation of funeral customs is necessary, not only out of duty to one's parents, but also to establish family status in the village or community. There is competition among families for the most elaborate funerals. As a result, Chinese families often go deeply into debt to pay for the costs of priests, mourners, sacrificial objects, wreaths and flowers, firecrackers, brass bands, coffin, gravesite, and a public feast for kinfolk, friends and neighbors.

Two Examples of Chinese Funerals

The funeral of a wealthy man in pre-communist China, as described by an American scholar,[14] included:

>   Hundreds of condolence scrolls
>
>   100 marching soldiers with rifles
>
>   30 policemen
>
>   Portable pavilions trimmed with porcelain vases and other
>   valuable works of art
>
>   Paid mourners
>
>   A heavy coffin with 15 pallbearers

Despite the official disapproval of expensive funerals, considered wasteful and superstitious by the Communists, this family tradition persists today. The funeral of the father of a Communist Party member named Liu was reported (with disapproval) in the Hunan Province press in 1978. The three sons invited a Daoist priest to conduct the funeral, and to pick a proper time and place for the funeral and burial, which was described as follows:

> *... the coffin was covered with a cloth and a photograph.... Some fifty to sixty wreaths were carried in front of the coffin.... Musicians played drums and gongs in front and behind. Some three*

14. D. C. Graham, "Folk Religion in Southwest China," Smithsonian Institution, Misc. Collections, Vol. 142, No. 2, 1961.

hundred people attended the funeral.... The funeral procession passed two communes, four production brigades, and fourteen production teams....

During the journey the Liu family also distributed money to passers-by.... On the day of the burial forty tables of food were set up for lunch. Some thousand catties of grain and three hundred catties of pork [about 600 lbs.] were wasted. Expenses reached 790 yuan [about $400].... Liu also exploited his position and power to order a vehicle and tractor to take his relatives and friends to the funeral.... He accepted more than seventy scrolls and over 420 feet of cloth from the people who attended the funeral.[15]

CHINESE FESTIVALS TO REMEMBER THE DEAD

In traditional Chinese life, every month had its festival, celebrated both with religious rites and with family and community feasting. The festival celebration was always a group activity, and strengthened the family and community ties. Two festivals with strong religious and family significance were: Ch'ing-ming (Qing-ming), on the third day of the third month of the lunar calendar; and the Feast of the Souls, on the fifteenth day of the seventh month.

The Feast of the Souls, like our Halloween or All Souls Day, is based on concern for the souls of the dead. The entire community goes to the Buddhist temples to burn incense and attend special services for all homeless spirits.

The Ch'ing Ming festival, in contrast, is a family day. Families go together to the graves of the ancestors—usually located in wasteland on the edge of the fields—to pull the weeds, clean up the debris from the winter, and to offer sacrifices of food and drink, which are later eaten by the family. This springtime festival becomes both a time for a family picnic and for remembering and honoring the ancestors. By performing these rituals, the family makes sure that the ancestors will not become abandoned spirits like those remembered on the day of the Feast of Souls.

CONCLUSION

Many of these customs persist in China today. They have virtually disappeared in the cities, but they persist in the countryside where 80 percent of the people live. It is certain that the Confucian heritage, the honoring of the ancestors, and the central value of family continuity remain. Filial piety is a moral imperative, binding parents and children in death as in life.

15. H. Welch, "The Fate of Religion" in *The China Difference*, Ross Terrill, ed., Harper & Row, 1979.

LESSON REVIEW

QUESTIONS FOR DISCUSSION

Select the most appropriate questions.

1. Discuss the students' personal experience of death, funerals, grieving, and family remembrance of deceased grandparents or relatives.

2. Do their families observe memorial customs for departed loved ones? How is their memory preserved? Do they visit the graves? Do they keep family genealogical records and discuss family roots?

3. Compare some Chinese and Western observances at the time of death: e.g., funerals, family memorial customs, cemetery services, wakes, etc.

4. What are the positive values of the Chinese customs on honoring the ancestors and the family elders? Discuss the growing problem of caring for the elderly in our fragmented and mobile American society. What can we learn from the Chinese experience?

5. Compare traditional Chinese funerals with a simple memorial service without religious rituals or significance. Recall for the class the funeral of John F. Kennedy, viewed on nationwide TV by millions of Americans. Are there values in traditional funeral rituals and customs?

6. Consider the death and burial of a homeless person in a city like New York, without the presence of a single friend or family member. Why is this more tragic than ordinary death in a family and community?

7. Discuss the quotation from Kastenbaum:

   To accept death means to take charge of one's life.... The thought of death urges one to assume a total plan for his life. The vitality of death leads one to adopt an ideal or goal, a noble life, or a major achievement as the purpose of existence. Through the vitality of death, one is able to see all events in life from the perspective of his total existence.

9. Discuss this quotation from an American writer:

   The great tragedy is not death itself but death without meaning. The greater tragedy may be life without meaning.

CLASS ASSIGNMENT

1. Write an essay discussing the similarities and differences between Mao Zedong's views of life and death, and those of the Confucianists and the Chinese Buddhists.

2. Alternate assignment: Interview parents or grandparents, asking them to describe funeral customs, grieving, and memorial customs for deceased family members.

W·O·R·K·S·H·E·E·T

VOCABULARY REVIEW FOR LESSON 10
Coping with Death in China

Name _____ Period _____ Date _____

Define the following terms:

ancestral tablets _____

_____

cremation _____

_____

cult _____

_____

genealogy _____

_____

heritage _____

_____

incense _____

_____

immortality _____

_____

kowtow _____

_____

mourner _____

_____

mortician _____

_____

pallbearer _____

_____

rituals, rites _____

_____

secularism _____

_____

spirit, soul _____

_____

salvation _____

_____

yoga _____

_____

LESSON 11

Maoist Values

LESSON PURPOSE

This lesson will describe what has been called the "Maoist vision" for a new person and new society. By Maoist values we mean the radical changes in social structures, class relationships, and personal morality that constituted the goals of the Maoist leadership. Students will compare Chinese communitarian values with American individualism and personal values. The context is China's need to feed and sustain over one billion people.

INTRODUCTION

There was a time during the 1970s when visitors returning from China reported a country that seemed to have found solutions to many of the problems facing our own societies in the West. They saw a nation of nearly one billion people that was attempting to provide food, housing, schools, health care, employment, and the basic necessities of life for its people without the gross inequities that seemed inevitable elsewhere. There was no crime in the streets, no drug problem; they saw no beggars, homeless derelicts, or pornography. The streets were clean, the people were honest, and the children were healthy.

For visitors who had known the old China, the most vivid impressions were the changes in attitudes, values, and the spirit of the people. For example, James Reston, senior editor of *The New York Times*, writing in 1971, was overwhelmed by "the staggering thing that modern China is trying to do. They're not trying merely to revolutionize people, and establish a sense of social conscience, but they're really trying to change the character of these people. The place is one vast school of moral philosophy." Reston went on to say, "I was struck by the tremendous effort to bring out what is best in people, what makes them good, what makes them cooperate with one another and be considerate and not beastly to one another. They are trying to do that."[1]

Harrison Salisbury, a well-known journalist with wide experience in China and Asia, wrote this in 1973.

> *There is—at least for a time—a New Chinese Man and a New Chinese Woman. They have self-respect and dignity. They*

1. J. Reston, *The New York Times*, Sept. 1, 1971.

were admirable in their fellowship, kindness and sense of self-sacrifice.... I had convinced myself that there was in China a new spirit among men, a contagious spirit, one on which China could build.[2]

INDIVIDUAL RIGHTS IN A COMMUNITARIAN SOCIETY

Since the revelations about the "ten bad years" of the Cultural Revolution (1966–1976) became known in the West, journalists and others have looked beneath the surface impressions of China and have published more critical views on what they saw and heard in China. While it is true that the restructuring of society and the economy in China has brought about remarkable improvements meeting the daily needs and quality of life for the people of China, these writers have reported examples of restrictions on individual freedoms which Americans would find intolerable.

For example, Chinese peasants are not allowed to freely migrate to the cities, writers are not allowed to freely publish criticism of government, and there is no true democratic participation in politics as we understand it. Books such as Fox Butterfield's *China: Alive in the Bitter Sea* contain stories, statistics and interviews which indicate that China is no utopia. Ross Terrill, author of several books on China, wrote this in 1983.

> *There is a gap between China's image and what China is really like. It existed long before the era of good feelings of the 1970s, and, in a way, it still exists.... There are rich and fascinating layers of Chinese life that survive and transcend the dead hand of the Communist system; the Chinese are as skilled at presenting these to the foreigner as they are at preserving them from any profound politicization. Whatever this tells us about Chinese stoicism and the superficiality of Marxism's grip on Chinese minds, it makes the foreign observer's task of aligning the political and nonpolitical realms of Chinese life a tricky one.*[3]

American images of China have changed dramatically since the time of the Korean War and the "bamboo curtain." Yet we tend to judge China by American standards. While we can justifiably object to violations of human rights and the lack of democratic participation, we need to understand the enormous logistical problems posed by a population of over one billion. The restrictions on migration into the cities, for example, prevent the chaotic flood of impoverished peasants that inundates most third world cities. Instead, China seeks to improve the standard of living for the rural people. The harsh "one-child family" population policy must be seen in the same context.

2. H. Salisbury, *To Peking and Beyond: A Report on the New Asia*, New York: Quadrangle, 1973, p. 301.
3. R. Terrill, *Atlantic*, Oct. 1983.

Since this lesson series focuses on religion and values, we will deal only with the nonpolitical realm of Chinese life, leaving politics and ideology for other studies. This lesson will compare Western concepts of the rights of the individual with Chinese communitarianism, both traditional and contemporary. American students should compare their own emphasis on personal career goals, self-realization, and "do your own thing," with the Chinese sense of community, social responsibilities, and obligation to family, society and nation, looking for the strengths and weaknesses of each.

ONE BILLION PEOPLE: THE PROBLEM OF SURVIVAL

"Democracy Wall" flourished briefly in 1978 and 1979 in Peking, with counterparts in other cities. Hundreds of hand-written wall posters set forth the opinions and grievances of individuals. Mimeographed newspapers published by small groups of young intellectuals were widely distributed. Today, only official newspapers and periodicals are permitted, and most Chinese are cautious about talking too freely with foreign visitors.

The leaders of the Chinese government, as they have in past ages, require what they call a "united front" of all the people. To them, it is perfectly reasonable to expect the citizens to put national goals before personal wishes. China's leaders, conscious of the desperate race between population growth and increased production of food and consumer goods, have set the target of "full modernization by the year 2,000." For a nation of over one billion, this may be the only means to survival; land and resources need to be rationally allocated to produce the food and other necessities required to sustain life.

Yet even the Communist leaders have recently relaxed the central planning process, having discovered that the profit incentive and personal initiative can enhance production. It is this experimentation, combining socialist methods with imported and traditional concepts of free enterprise, that makes China today both dynamic and fascinating. Will this enormous experiment succeed? As the economist Barbara Ward has said, "we should all hope and pray that it will, for if it doesn't, there is little the rest of the world can do to help."

In his book, *An Inquiry into the Human Prospect*, the American economist, Robert Heilbroner, raised the fundamental question facing mankind today: "Is there hope for survival in the years ahead?" In his analysis, the human predicament has led to the loss of hope. The persistence of global inflation, poverty, hunger, waste of resources, environmental overload, pollution, inequities between the rich and poor, population pressures, wars, and racial hatred contribute to the sense of despair. In a pessimistic mood, he wrote that, in his view, "only an authoritarian, or possibly only a revolutionary regime, will be capable of mounting the immense task of social reorganization needed to escape catastrophe."[4]

This lesson will raise questions for reflection and discussion on how to deal with these matters of human survival, while preserving traditional human values.

MAO: HIS BACKGROUND

During the warlord period (1916–1928), the central government fell apart and the countryside lapsed into semi-anarchy. The Chinese people, particularly the peasants who still number over 80 percent of the population, suffered from landlord/warlord oppression, civil war, banditry, famine, and other miseries. Both the Kuomintang and Communist parties worked toward the goal of national salvation—unification of the nation and social and economic security for the people.

Like many other young patriots, Mao Zedong was born in a peasant village and knew first-hand the rigors and suffering of the rural people. He became not only a guerrilla leader and Marxist revolutionary, but an

4. R. Heilbroner, *An Inquiry into the Human Prospect*, New York: Norton, 1974.

idealist, seeking social and political reforms that would liberate the people from the endemic problems that plagued their lives. Like most patriots of his time, he identified the two major obstacles to national salvation as: (1) the domination of the people by a power elite, the land-lord/gentry class; and (2) the occupation of China by the imperialist powers. He identified these as the "twin mountains" carried on the backs of the Chinese people. He believed that only by mobilizing the urban and rural working class people, could they achieve liberation from these burdens. He said, "The people, and the people alone, are the motive force in history."

In his *Report on an Investigation of the Peasants' Movement in Hunan Province* (1927), he described what he called the four systems of authority that dominated the peasants: (1) the corrupt government system at all levels; (2) the family/clan system; (3) the supernatural system (local religions) "ranging from the King of Hell down to the village gods"; and (4) the oppression of women by men. He saw the whole feudal-patriarchal system as "four thick ropes" binding the Chinese people.

MAO: HIS VISION

Mao's life (1893–1976) bridged the modern history of China, from the final years of the decaying Manchu empire, through the years of semi-anarchy and civil strife, to the final victory of his forces in 1949. He spent years of his adult life living among the peasants, witnessing their misery. Most of them were sharecroppers or tenant farmers, tilling land that averaged two to three acres per family, and existing precariously at a bare subsistence level. Millions of them died prematurely in those years from hunger, illness, and poverty. Three to six million died in a single three-province famine in 1928–1930. It was Mao's vision to bring some measure of security into the lives of these people.

This required the restructuring of the forces of production, and (he believed) a transformation of people's traditional attitudes, values, and morality. The major change in the mode of production was collectivizing agriculture. Land was seized from the landlords in an often brutal nationwide campaign, and all private farms were combined into over 50,000 rural people's communes; these were divided into brigades and production teams, each the size of a small village.

SCHOOLS AND MEDICAL CARE

In the past thirty-four years, the average life-span in China has nearly doubled, from 35 to 67. This is due largely to better nutrition and health care.

With universal primary education, people now can read publications on proper health care methods and modern farming methods, as well as many other technical books and manuals. The number of schools has more than tripled since 1949, and the number of students in school has risen from 25,776,000 to 199,066,000 in 1982. Even so, the number of illiterates and semi-illiterates above age 12 in 1982 was still 235 million, or one-fourth of the total population. Less than half the students in primary schools could go on to junior and senior high school, due to the shortage of schools and teachers.

As for college-level education, by comparison with Western countries, China still has far to go. Less than four percent of high school graduates can go on for higher education. The proportion of students at schools beyond high school per 10,000 people is 11.4 in China, 58.4 in India, 106 in USSR, 210 in Japan, and 507 in the United States.[5]

A major achievement has been the virtual elimination of epidemic diseases that periodically took thousands of lives, and others (such as malaria) which sapped the strength of millions. An American physician, Dr. George Hatem, who has lived and worked in China for fifty years, recently described the remarkable achievement in the control of diseases. He took part in the great campaigns in the 1950s that eradicated the acute communicable diseases, such as smallpox, cholera, and bubonic plague. Later, the endemic diseases such as malaria, tuberculosis, schistosomiasis, venereal diseases, and kala-azar were brought under control. Finally, he became a leader in the campaign against leprosy, which infected an estimated 500,000 people in 1949. Now the figure has dropped to less than 200,000, all of whom receive modern treatment on an outpatient basis, rather than confinement to leper colonies.[6]

The key to the success of these campaigns against disease was the collective mobilization of the people. For example, schistosomiasis is a dread disease in which a parasite infects and bloats the human body, eventually causing a painful death. These parasites are transmitted through the feces of infected humans, carried by freshwater snails, and reinfect humans who wade barefoot in the rice paddies. The disease was eliminated by mobilizing thousands of people along the banks of streams, lakes, and rice paddies to dig out and destroy the snails. The rice farmers of south China need no longer fear this dreaded disease.

Other nationwide campaigns mobilized all the people to eliminate the "four pests": school children had contests to bring in dead bedbugs, flies, mosquitoes, and rat tails. Because of the food they consume, pet dogs and cats were forbidden. Students volunteered during summer vacations to work in the fields, planting, weeding, and harvesting the crops.

In all of the campaigns and projects, the Chinese people were mobilized collectively. Teams worked in the fields. Very few students went on to college and other careers. There was no place for the lone individual pursuing his own interests apart from the group.

5. "Facts and Figures: Education," *Beijing Review*, Oct. 3, 1983, p. 26.
6. "China's Contributions to Leprosy Control," *Beijing Review*, Dec. 5, 1983.

Mao sought to change the basic motivation, from private profit to working for the needs of all. Slogans such as "Fight Selfishness" and "Serve the People" were promoted by films, dramas, and campaigns to emulate selfless heroes. The people studied and memorized the writings of Mao.

HERO MODELS: SERVE THE PEOPLE

One of Mao's writings, "In Memory of Norman Bethune," memorialized a Canadian medical doctor who died of blood poisoning while performing battlefront surgery during the Anti-Japanese War. Because of Mao's essay, he became a model for selfless service:

> *Comrade Bethune's spirit, his utter devotion to others without any thought of self, was shown in his boundless sense of responsibility in his work and his boundless warm-heartedness towards all the people. Every Communist must learn from him. There are not a few people who are irresponsible in their work, shoving the heavy loads onto others and choosing the easy ones for themselves. At every turn they think of themselves before others. When they make some small contribution, they swell with pride and brag about it.... No one who returned from the fighting front failed to express admiration for Dr. Bethune.... We must all learn the spirit of absolute selflessness from him. With this spirit everyone can be very useful, to the people. A man's ability may be great or small, but if he has this spirit, he is already noble-minded and pure, a man of moral integrity and above common interests, a man who is of value to the people.*[7]

Long before the Communists, Chinese teachers and parents used stories of famous emperors, magistrates, and filial children to teach moral values to the young people. Posters, songs, magazine and newspaper stories, films and dramas of contemporary hero models are used to teach Maoist values. (Refer to the short play, *Do Not Spit at Random*, found on page 99 of the Primary Sources section.) In recent years, nationwide campaigns lifted up a single hero for emulation by all children. These heroes, usually young men or women, are selfless, hardworking, and devoted to serving their comrades and their country. They are courageous, braving dangers, and often giving their lives to save others.

One of these was Ouyang Hai, age 23, a squad leader in the army. He died while pushing a horse loaded with ammunition out of the path of a train, saving the train loaded with his comrades. *The Song of Ouyang Hai*, widely read by China's youth, commemorates this young hero. (Excerpts of *The Song of Ouyang Hai* can be found in the Primary Source section, on page 98.)

7. "In Memory of Norman Bethune," Dec.1939, in *Five Articles by Mao Tse-tung*, Beijing, Foreign Language Press, 1968.

Other heroes include farmers, sailors, factory workers, and children. A 12-year-old girl dies while pushing her cow out of the path of a train. A farmer drowns while rescuing a neighbor from a water-filled pit. In his brief 21 years, a young man named Mai Xiande did the following:

1. Did all the dirty work in camp for his friends while on a fishing trip.

2. Saved a ton and a half of grain from his commune's flooded storehouse by wading chest-deep through tidal waters and loading a boat single-handedly.

3. Battled against the in-rushing tide to repair a breach in a sea dike.

4. Won six citations in two years on civilian militia duty.

5. Received praise for using his own body to block a leak in his ship during naval exercises.

6. Remained at his post in the ship's engine room for three hours after receiving critical wounds from shrapnel entering his brain.[8]

8. From *China Reconstructs*, Dec. 1966, pp. 45-46.

LESSON REVIEW

QUESTIONS FOR DISCUSSION

The main focus of the discussion will be to raise the question of personal rights versus responsibility to others. Without condoning the abuses of human rights in China in past years, help the students to see the enormous logistical problems posed by a population of over one billion on approximately the same land area as the United States. In many ways the situations of the two countries are not comparable.

1. Discuss the problem of feeding over one billion people—nearly one quarter of the human race—with only seven percent of the world's arable land.

2. Can you think of examples in the U.S. which compare with China's mass campaigns to eliminate epidemic diseases? How would Americans respond to such campaigns of mass volunteer service?

3. Discuss the difference between America's free enterprise system with the planned economy of China. Note the government regulations and agencies which control even our "free enterprise" system, particularly with regard to toxic wastes, pollution controls, soil erosion, food and drug controls, aircraft safety, etc.

4. Compare American individualism with Chinese communitarianism. Are Americans too self-centered and individualistic? Discuss ways in which Americans could improve our country by working together, by cooperating in projects and programs, particularly at local levels.

5. Discuss the sacrifice of personal desires for the larger goals of the family or nation.

6. Discuss the dilemma of a country like ours that gives precedence to personal rights and freedoms, democracy, and due process of law. Criminals and others take advantage of the loopholes in our system, while an authoritarian system like China's can override the rights of the individual in order to wipe out a social problem like the use and sale of illegal drugs.

CLASS ACTIVITIES

1. Copy and distribute the excerpt from *The Song of Ouyang Hai* on page 98, and read it to the class. Discuss the character of Ouyang Hai and the use of hero models in China as examples of selflessness and service to others.

2. Prepare and perform the one-act play, *Do Not Spit at Random*, found on page 99. As an alternate option, ask the students to write their own one-act "morality play," basing it in contemporary America.

CLASS ASSIGNMENT

1. Ask the students to list the persons (public figures) past and present whom they most admire, and to identify the qualities they admire in these persons. Make a second list of admirable persons they know personally (family members, friends, etc.).

2. Copy, distribute, and read "The Most Admired Persons Poll" found in Primary Sources on page 103. Read two or three of the students' papers from the assignment above. Ask the students to identify the qualities they admire in the persons listed in their papers, and write these on the chalkboard. Compare their listing with the "Most Admired Persons" list, and with the Chinese hero models.

W·O·R·K·S·H·E·E·T

VOCABULARY REVIEW FOR LESSON 11
Maoist Values

Name _____ Period _____ Date _____

Define the following terms:

human rights _____

_____

communitarian _____

_____

profit incentive _____

_____

global inflation _____

_____

anarchy _____

_____

landlord/gentry class _____

_____

feudal/patriarchal system _____

_____

agricultural collectives _____

_____

people's communes _____

_____

epidemic disease _____

_____

endemic disease _____

_____

parasites _____

_____

collectivizing _____

_____

mobilized _____

_____

utopia _____

_____

LESSON 12

Family Life and the Status of Women

LESSON PURPOSE

Population pressures on land, resources, and human relationships have forced the Chinese government to impose harsh measures aimed at stabilizing the population. In this lesson we will examine the changes in the status of women, the strains on family life, and the experimental policies and programs designed to cope with these problems.

POPULATION, LAND, AND FOOD

Grain production in China more than tripled in the thirty years between 1950 and 1980—from 100 million tons, to 318 million tons. But in the same period the population nearly doubled—from 500 million to almost one billion. Since grain—wheat and corn in the north, rice in the south—is the main source of food in China, the average diet scarcely improved.

During those same years, the average area of cultivated land dropped from .4 acre to .24 acre per person. New factories, roads, irrigation projects, and housing were built over scarce cropland, while demands increased on the food supply, resulting from two "baby booms."

The population increase in the past thirty years was extraordinary. By 1980, there were 122 million women of reproductive age (20–49), whose average birth rate was 2.3 babies. If this rate continues unchecked, China's population will rise to 1.3 billion by the end of this century, and one hundred years from now it will exceed 2.5 billion.

Better nutrition and health care are the primary reasons for the population explosion. In earlier centuries, China's population took more than one thousand years to double from 50 to 100 million. From the year 2 A.D. to 1290, the growth rate was virtually zero. Between 1950 and 1970, China's annual growth rate soared from an earlier rate never exceeding 0.31 percent, to an unprecedented 2.6 percent. However, under the influence of a national family planning program, the growth rate began to drop in 1971, reaching a low of 1.2 percent in 1980.

Even that lower rate of growth will eventually cancel out the gains in standard of living set forth in the goals of the Four Modernizations. Official policy now aims to contain population growth so that it will not exceed 1.2 billion by the end of the century. This requires a natural rate of increase of under 1 percent. These are the reasons behind the "one-child family" campaign.

FAMILY LIFE TODAY: THE ONE-CHILD FAMILY

The family is still the keystone of Chinese society today. Families are stable, the divorce rate is low, and traditional values continue to hold families together. Since children are legally responsible to care for their aging parents, most grandparents live with their children in three-generation families.

Nevertheless, great changes are taking place in Chinese family life. Many more women are working outside the home. Many young children spend much of their time in daycare centers. Perhaps the most profound changes are coming with the reduced number of children. If the one-child family becomes the norm, there is danger of a nation of spoiled children who have no experience of brothers and sisters. Even worse, there are stories of husband-wife tensions over the birth of a baby girl, of female infanticide, and of forced abortions.

Special incentives are used to encourage families to accept the one-child family. The rewards include free medical care for the child; priority admission to nurseries, kindergartens, and primary schools; larger apartments; bonuses for city workers, and increased work points; and larger private plots and better housing for peasants. Severe penalties are imposed for one-child families who break their contracts. All benefits must be returned, salaries will be reduced, and all costs for a third child must be borne by the parents. Promotions may be withheld, and mothers may lose their jobs.

Opposition to the one-child family policy is seen particularly in the rural areas, where large families and male children are not only traditional, but also desirable for economic reasons. More able-bodied farm workers mean higher family incomes.

THE STATUS OF WOMEN

Women in old China suffered in many ways. Placed in a subservient role in the Confucian social structure, married into their husband's family, deprived of education and job opportunities by a male-dominated culture, they were largely confined to the home. In parts of China, they worked in the fields alongside the men. Footbinding, the cruel custom which prevailed even into the twentieth century, hobbled higher class women and kept them at home. Even so, it has often been said that women have been, in fact, the real heads of household in Chinese families, supervising the housekeeping affairs and the raising of the children.

Women's rights to marry freely, to vote, own property, and be educated became national issues after the 1911 Republican Revolution. During the war against Japan, women played larger roles, particularly in the Communist areas. The 1950 Marriage Law for the first time legally prohibited bigamy, concubinage, and child betrothal, while making husbands and wives equal partners. Women gained the right to own property, to sue for divorce, and to take a job outside the home. But to this day, women in China continue to fight for full implementing of the Marriage Law.

Household tasks are still carried out primarily by women, whether working at other jobs or not. Women are a minority at all levels of leadership, from national government down to factory and village committees, and men still predominate in middle and upper level jobs in industry and the professions.

DIVORCE AND MEDIATION

Most civil disputes in China are handled by mediation, not by the courts. China has only 15,000 lawyers, compared to 581,000 in the United States. Nearly one million mediation committees handle everything from juvenile crime to disputes between neighbors and family arguments. In 1983, Chinese lawyers handled only 37,000 civil cases, while neighborhood mediation committees resolved 6,978,000 cases. Mediation seems to work in China because Chinese are sensitive to the opinions of their neighbors.

In a typical marriage dispute, a mediation committee in Canton dealt with the case of a factory worker, Li Junan, who began beating his wife during their quarrels. She packed up and went back to her mother. The mediation committee visited Mr. Li and, despite his hostility, talked with him for several hours. As a result, Mr. Li agreed to treat his wife properly and she returned home. The couple was reunited, and a divorce avoided.*

In another divorce case, heard by a people's court, we have an example of the court, the lawyers, and the judges doing their best to keep the marriage together. In the end, the court decided that reconciliation could not bring happiness, and the divorce was granted. This story, "Mediation Settles a Divorce Case," can be found in the Primary Sources section on page 105.

LIFE WITHOUT A SON

Despite the logic (on a national scale) of limiting the size of families, Chinese tradition decrees that each family shall have a son, for it is through the sons that the family name is carried on through the generations. In addition, it is the sons who provide old age security for the

*From "Chinese Say, Don't Sue, Mediate," *New York Times*, April 12, 1984, p. 2.

parents, since the married daughters traditionally move in with their in-law families. The burden and blame fall on the women when they bear a daughter instead of a son.

"Life Without a Son" is a letter published in *People's Daily* from rural women living in Anhui Province. It discusses the shame and frustration they face from having families with only daughters and no sons. This letter is reprinted in the Primary Sources section, on page 107.

THE "FIVE GOODS"

Model families are elected by their neighbors to be honored as "Five Goods Families." In 1983, there were 3.8 million such model families in China. The "five goods" required of a family are: diligent work and study; consideration for the family members and the neighbors; careful family planning and attention to children's education; observance of law and discipline; and courteous public behavior.

In Shanghai, over 41,000 families have been selected for this honor. An example of a "Five Goods Family"—from the Chenjiaqiao neighborhood in Shanghai—shows how a family that once had its own domestic problems was helped by the neighborhood committee to reform itself so that now it has been chosen as a model family. This story, "Between Older and Younger Generations," can be found in the Primary Sources section on page 108.

LESSON REVIEW

QUESTIONS FOR DISCUSSION

1. Discuss China's dilemma: limited arable land, and a huge, growing population.

2. Discuss the pros and cons of three-generation families. Ask if any students have grandparents living in their homes, or nearby. If not, how often do they see them and what is their relationship?

3. Discuss the role of the neigborhood committees, and the handling of civil cases by mediation instead of in the courts. Would this system work in the United States?

4. Discuss the status of women in China and the U.S.: education, jobs, and their role in the family.

5. Discuss the campaign for "Five Goods Families." Would this work in the United States?

CLASS ACTIVITY: Population, Food and Space

The purpose of this activity is to demonstrate the human pressures resulting from overcrowding.

Clear a space in the room that will barely hold 25 persons. One person represents 40 million people. Using the following chart, which accurately follows the population growth in China from the year 1400 A.D., ask the students to stand together, one group after the other. The first two or three groups will not feel crowded; this symbolizes China in earlier centuries. The final group of 25 will be jammed together, symbolizing life in a densely populated country like China today.

				TOTAL
Group 1	China in 1400	80 million	2 persons	2
Group 2	China in 1600	150 million	2 more persons	4
Group 3	China in 1850	450 million	7 more persons	11
Group 4	China in 1970	800 million	9 more persons	20
Group 5	China in 1982	1 billion	5 more persons	25

CLASS ACTIVITY: The Case of the Stolen Bicycle

The purpose of this activity is to role play the mediating function of a neighborhood committee in the case of a stolen bicycle.

A 12-year-old boy was seen by his neighbors to have a new bicycle. Knowing that his father had died and that his mother was supporting three children by working in a textile factory sewing garments, the neighborhood committee chairman came to make inquiries. When the boy could not explain where he got the bicycle, they checked with the police and discovered it had been stolen from a family on the next street over.

The neighborhood committee then meets with the boy and his mother. Later, they meet privately to discuss how best to handle the case. Ask the students to make a decision that will be best for the boy and his family, as well as for upholding law and order.

(Note: This activity is based on an actual case, in which the committee's decision was to find a part-time job for the boy so that he could save his money and eventually buy a bicycle.)

FOR OPTIONAL STUDY

The following curriculum may be obtained, which includes six lessons with activities exploring the meaning of hunger, and the relationship between hunger and development issues. Students must choose among different development policies, and evaluate the effects of their decisions in a hypothetical developing nation.

Food for All: Teaching Against Hunger
Intercom, Global Perspectives in Education, Inc.
218 East 18th Street
New York, NY 10003

W·O·R·K·S·H·E·E·T

Family Life in China

Name _____ Period _____ Date _____

Define the following terms:

"baby boom" _____

_____

bigamy _____

_____

"five goods" _____

_____

child betrothal _____

_____

concubinage _____

_____

footbinding _____

_____

infanticide _____

_____

mediation _____

_____

one-child family _____

_____

reconciliation _____

_____

subservient _____

_____

LESSON 13

Chinese Youth: What Is the Meaning of Life?

LESSON PURPOSE

The purpose of this lesson is twofold: (1) to introduce American students to the current life experience, attitudes, and values of Chinese youth; and (2) to stimulate American students to reflect on the meaning of life, and their own goals and values.

SOURCE MATERIALS FOR THIS LESSON

The primary source materials for this lesson were originally published in the national magazine *Chinese Youth* (Zhongguo Qingnian) in 1980. Thousands of letters poured in to the magazine in response to a letter writen by Pan Xiao, a despairing young woman who asked the question, "What is the meaning of life?"

The young letter-writers offered two basically opposing answers to her question. One group of writers, cynical and disillusioned after suffering bad experiences during the Cultural Revolution, are remarkably candid about criticizing the official goals and values. One young man writes, "Is there anyone who is not an idiot who does not desire great wealth, a high position, and a beautiful wife?" Another believes that "the path of life means money, position, and personal happiness."

Others remain true to the ideals of selfless service through collective action. Pan Xiao is criticized for having given up her original high ideals and commitments. They, too, had suffered hardships and witnessed injustices; all the more reason (they write) to continue the struggle together to achieve the goals of "the four modernizations," and a better life for all.

THE CULTURAL REVOLUTION (1966–1976)

Pan Xiao, the 23-year-old writer of this now-famous letter, is one of millions of Chinese youth today—over 600 million under age 30. What are their goals in life? How do they view the government's new policies to stimulate production based on economic incentives and profit motives, in contrast to the Maoist vision for egalitarian sharing and selfless service to the nation and the people? In those years, "careerism" (pursuing one's own career goals) was considered a moral crime.

These letters were written by members of China's "lost generation," the young people, most of them teenagers, who stopped studying in 1966 when all the schools closed down for a period of three or more years. Millions of them volunteered for hardship work assignments in remote villages in distant provinces, responding to Chairman Mao's call to "Serve the people" and to "Learn from the peasants." Mao believed that intellectuals, students, professors, government officials, and others from the privileged classes should learn what life is like for those who work at manual labor. Young volunteers went off to frontier villages in teams, sent off at the train stations in Shanghai and other coastal cities by friends, relatives, and brass bands.

Many of these young people never returned to complete their education. By the time the schools reopened, a new generation of students was ready to fill the limited spaces. For this reason, the Cultural Revolution age group is today often called the lost generation. Many of them returned to the cities where unemployed youth are now a big problem. In recent years, under more permissive government policies, some of them have opened small restaurants, shoe repair shops, photo studios, and other private enterprises; others remain unemployed. Many of those who had dreams of going on for a college education and a professional career are bitter and disillusioned.

PAN XIAO'S DESPAIR

One of those is Pan Xiao. Here is how she begins her letter:*

> I am now twenty-three years old. It should be said that for me life has just begun. But it seems that all the mystery and attraction of life no longer exist and I have already reached its end. Looking back on my journey, it has been a trip from crimson to gray, a trip from hope through disappointment to despair, a long river of ideology originating at a selfless source and terminating with the self as center.

Pan Xiao describes how her own values and commitments were formed from reading stories of labor heroes and famous Chinese leaders. She became convinced that to serve the people and the nation was the highest goal in life.

> I read by chance a pamphlet entitled "For Whom Should One Live and How Should One Act?" I read it again and again. I began to form my ... view of life: to live is to make others live

*From *Zhongguo Qingnian*, 1980, No. 5.

even better; to live one must have lofty ideals and be ready to dedicate all one has to the needs of the Party and people. I lost myself in a passion of dedication. I wrote in my diary whole paragraphs of dazzling words and tried to model myself on heroes in everything I did or said.

Later, during the Cultural Revolution, she saw violence and human behavior that contrasted sharply with these ideals.

I was puzzled; I began to feel things around me did not appear as attractive as they had in books I had read previously. I asked myself: Should I believe the books or my eyes? Should I trust teachers or myself?

Then she suffered a series of losses and disappointments in her own life. Her father-in-law died and her harmonious family broke into fighting over money matters. Her closest friend betrayed her, reporting their private conversations to the Party leadership. Her fiance abandoned her. She was forced to drop out of school and find a job. She searched for an answer to the meaning of life, consulting gray-haired old men, workers, peasants, and other young people. She read books by Chinese and European philosophers. But none of these gave her a satisfactory answer.

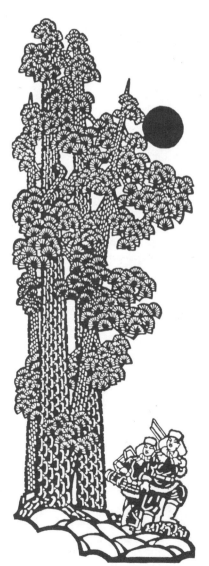

To live for the sake of revolution appears to be hollow and wide of the mark.... If we say one lives for fame, that would sound too remote for people in general. There are not many who "leave a good name for a hundred generations...." To say that one has to live for the whole of mankind would be irrelevant to reality.... If life means the pleasure of eating, drinking, and playing, then one becomes just a sojourner in the world, born with nothing but a bare body, and dying just bones and skin. That does not amount to much.

Many people have tried to persuade me to stop cudgeling my brains, saying: "Life is for the sake of living. Many people do not understand its meaning, but they lead a happy life just the same." But this won't do for me. I keep turning over in my mind [the questions of] life and meaning, as if a noose were tied around my neck, forcing me to make a decision right away.

Pan Xiao searched for a guide to the meaning of life, but couldn't find it.

Some say in this world there is a broad and great cause, but I have no idea where it is. Oh, the path of life, why is it ever narrowing as one walks along? As for myself, I am already so tired now. It seems that slackening for a moment would mean total destruction. Indeed, I did stealthily go to watch the service at a Catholic church. I struck upon the idea of cutting my hair and becoming a nun. I even went so far as to consider putting an end to my life—I am extremely confused and self-contradictory.

She concludes her letter by asking the editor to publish her letter so that young people all over the country can read it. "Perhaps I can get some help from them," she said.

YOUTH VOLUNTEER SERVICE TEAMS

In an effort to combat selfishness in society, China's leaders launched a "Socialist Ethics and Courtesy Month" in March, 1982. The purpose is to promote courtesy and a spirit of generous service toward other persons. One result has been the organizing of volunteer youth service teams to combat the idea that "money is everything." In the city of Hangzhou, young workers in the Hangzhou Bicycle Factory organized over fifty volunteer service teams to help others. Once a week, they turned out to trim hair, take photos, repair bicycles and household appliances free of charge. In two years, they repaired over 12,000 bicycles for people, often going to their homes to save the nuisance of going a long way for a small repair.

The following year over 1,000 volunteer service teams were set up throughout the city, bringing help to thousands of families—especially the childless elderly, the sick, and the disabled. In China, these people are guaranteed a living by the government, but many find it difficult to keep up with household chores.

Volunteer youth teams made a survey and determined which households needed special help. Team members visit these households regularly to help with the household chores, washing, cooking, and shopping. One example is Chen Ahua, an 85-year-old woman who lost her husband when she was thirty-two, and then lost her young child. She had supported herself working as a housekeeper, but when she got too old for that, in 1964 she began living on government support.

A youth service team from the Hangzhou Guangming Silk Mill began to care for this old woman. They visit her two or three times a week, helping her wash clothes, clean house and do her shopping. A young married woman living nearby visits her every day and cooks special foods for her at the time of festivals. There is now a close relationship with this once-lonely woman.

By the end of 1982, 1,269 service groups were helping 521 childless elders and sick or disabled people.

During the Second Socialist Ethics Month (March 1983), a campaign was launched to improve service in the department stores and railways. Sales clerks would be friendly, greet customers with a smile, and never become angry with questions. Punctuality, safety, and courtesy were criteria for workers in transportation. Medical personnel would treat the patients like their own family members, and upgrade their skills.

During that month, environmental sanitation and tree planting was organized. Over 4,000 young people in the city of Guangzhou set up stalls to trim hair, repair garments and appliances, motorcycles, clocks, and watches. Some made home calls to fix water taps and electric lights, free of charge. Public service units provided streetside medical checkups and legal advice.

THE FIVE STRESSES AND FOUR POINTS OF DECENCY

Socialist Ethics and Courtesy Month was part of a larger campaign called "Socialist Spiritual Civilization." One Chinese writer recently pointed out the danger of over-emphasizing material values:

> Facts show that if one buries himself in economic construction to the neglect of building socialist spiritual civilization, he will run after material things and may even be interested only in material gains [personal profit]. Thus, he turns himself into a slave to material things, leading a rich, yet spiritually meaningless life....

To combat this trend toward neglect of spiritual values, China has adopted various campaigns, including the "Five Stresses" and the "Four Points of Decency."

The Five Stresses are: stress on decorum, manners, hygiene, discipline, and morals.

The Four Points of Decency are: (1) decency of the mind, meaning cultivating a proper ideology, moral character and integrity, and patriotism; (2) decency of language, which means the use of polite language; (3) decency of behavior, which means doing useful things for the people, working hard, showing concern for others, welfare, observing discipline, and safeguarding collective interests; (4) decency of environment, which includes paying attention to personal hygiene, and to sanitation at home and in public places.

LESSON REVIEW

CLASS ACTIVITY

Copy and distribute letter excerpts from *Chinese Youth*, found in Primary Sources on page 109. Use the Chinese letters to motivate American students to discuss Pan Xiao's question, "What is the meaning of life?"

Divide the students into five groups, according to topic headings:

Group 1   Letters of Sympathy and Encouragement for Pan Xiao

Group 2   Letters Supporting a Life Style of Selfless Service

Group 3   Letters That Say "Serve Yourself First"

Group 4   Letters Referring to Social Problems

Group 5   Letters Mentioning Duty to the Nation

Ask each group to read and discuss the letter excerpts under their topic heading. Choose one person to represent each group as a member of a five-person panel. Each panel member will present to the class reasons to support or to oppose the positions set forth by the Chinese letter writers. Open the floor to general discussion and debate. Ask the students to relate the five topic questions to the American context.

How would American youth respond to similar disappointments and broken dreams? How would they respond to an American "Pan Xiao," who wrote a similar letter to their school newspaper?

CLASS ASSIGNMENT

Convert the activity described above into an assignment, such as follows. Ask students to read and reflect on Pan Xiao's letter, and the letters in Group 3 (Letters That Say "Serve Yourself First"), and Group 2 (Letters Supporting a Life Style of Selfless Service). Have students write an essay in response, giving pros and cons for the various points of view put forth by the Chinese youth.

W·O·R·K·S·H·E·E·T

VOCABULARY FOR LESSON 13

Chinese Youth: What Is the Meaning of Life?

Name _____ Period _____ Date _____

Define the following terms:

egalitarian _____

_____

careerism _____

_____

ideology _____

_____

aspiration _____

_____

commitment _____

_____

"lost generation" _____

_____

selfless service _____

_____

Five Stresses _____

_____

Four Points of Decency _____

_____

cultural revolution _____

_____

Primary Sources

The Primary Sources are excerpted readings such as debates, stories, dramas, plays, letters and articles, most of which depict life, politics and religion in China. Primary Sources may be duplicated and distributed to the students as supplemental readings for the lessons in *Focus On China*. Refer to the lesson plan for specific recommendations on using them.

Contents of Primary Sources

CHINESE INVENTIONS TRANSMITTED TO THE WEST*

Chinese civilization was admired by the Europeans of the seventeenth and eighteenth centuries for the beauties of its silks and porcelains (chinaware), its painting and lacquerware, its philosophers and poets.

China's lack of progress in the nineteenth and twentieth centuries gave a false impression of Chinese scientific ability and ingenuity. The British scholar, Joseph Needham, in his seven-volume study *Science and Civilization in China*, has described countless Chinese inventions and scientific discoveries which became commonplace in China centuries before they were known in Europe. In this list the number following each item shows the number of centuries by which the Chinese invention and use preceded the European.

	Centuries in use before Europeans
Rotary fan and winnowing machine	14
Mechanical loom	4
Wheelbarrow (wheel in center; no load on person)	9
Efficient harness for draft animals (horse collar)	6
Crossbow (mass produced for Han Dynasty armies)	13
Deep drilling of wells	11
Cast iron	10
Iron-chain suspension bridge	10
Canal lock gates	7
Watertight compartments in shipbuilding	4
Sternpost rudder (replacing steering oar)	4
Paper money	4
Use of coal	4
Mechanical clock	6

*From Joseph Needham, *Science and Civilization in China*, Vol. I (Cambridge, 1954), p. 242.

THE CONFUCIAN DEBATE

Editor's Introduction

The teachings of Confucius were among the "four olds" (old ideas, old habits, old culture, old customs) attacked during the Cultural Revolution. Confucius was said to be an agent of the ruling class whose teachings were largely responsible for creating China's rigid class system dominated by an elite group with a monopoly of education, power and wealth. His teachings, they said, were designed to undergird the ruling class. For example, the teachings on benevolence and harmony, if practiced by the oppressed peasants, would prevent them from rising against the oppressors.

In the excerpts that follow, we read from a debate between Red Guards and Confucian scholars printed in *People's Daily* in 1967. In recent years the positive values in the teachings of Confucius have once again become acceptable.

"What Poison Was Spread by the Forum on Confucius*"

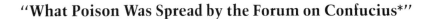

To let the public see clearly the vicious counter-revolutionary characteristics of these people, a few samples of their reactionary fallacies are as follows:

The Confucian scholars said:

The word "greatness" can be applied to Confucius unreservedly. Confucius was a great philosopher, statesman, and educator par excellence of the ancient world. It is by no means accidental that even today some of his theories radiate brilliance. Confucius was indeed the holiest and wisest of all philosophers. What Confucius said—even a word or two—has a bearing on the happiness of mankind.

Why does China have such an important position in the world? How did she come into being? ... Confucius, in my opinion, played a definite positive role. Just think, for as long as two thousand years and within a perimeter of tens of thousands of miles, people have generally regarded books compiled by Confucius as "the classics." Is that a trivial matter? As a matter of fact, people already had a unifying center, and have since developed a common language, common ideas, feelings, and living habits among themselves. Is this not of great importance to the formation of the solidarity of the Chinese nation?

Red Guard comment:

These people have lauded and glorified Confucius practically to the point of hysterical frenzy. Their object is all too clear. They want to establish the absolute authority of Confucius in the vain hope of using Confucian ideas and concepts to unify the thought, language, feelings,

*From the *People's Daily*, Peking, January 10, 1967.

and habits of 700 million people. They employ every conceivable means of disparaging and attacking Mao Tse-tung's thought, hoping thereby to induce a counter-revolutionary restoration. Under no circumstances should this be permitted to happen. We will certainly and thoroughly overthrow Confucian ideas and establish the absolute authority of Mao Tse-tung's thought!

The Confucian scholars said:

What is the highest criterion of politics? It is to conduct a "benevolent government"—"using moral virtues and the dictates of propriety as the criteria for judging people" until they "have a sense of shame and know the standards for comparison."

What is meant by self-restraint? ... The practice of the dictates of propriety, of course, entails respect for others and the treatment of people on an equal footing. It definitely does not lead to oppression and destruction and mass slaughter of other people.

The meaning of the word "benevolence" does not in any way merely imply "love of people." Rather, it means improving relationships between individuals.... It is to think of others at all times. Doesn't this mean "do as you would be done by"? Doesn't this imply "help others if you want to help yourself"? In this way, the relationships between one individual and another will not be any cause for complaint.

Red Guard comment:

The authority of the proletariat [the working people] can only give democracy to the people and impose authority over all reactionaries. Therefore the reactionaries denounce us for not being "benevolent." They want a "benevolent government" from us and that means doing away with proletarian authority. If their plots are successful, our Party and our country will be ruined and then the revolution will end in failure and the people will be doomed.

The Confucian scholars said:

In fact, what Confucius meant by "benevolence" *(ren)* ... [he] had all the people in mind. It is essentially characterized by "benevolence to the people." In plain language, "benevolence" means "love of people"—a recognition of man's right to survive. Before establishing one's own imperishable features, that is one's virtue, one's merit, and one's words, one should also help others to do so.... These words mean that before being good in all aspects, one should help others to do good too.

"Benevolence" means "to get along well with others." When individuals live in harmony, without deceiving each other but forgiving one another, then there is a state of loving and supporting one another.

While Confucius's "love of people" subjectively means to love the ruling class, in objective effect it means love of "the people."

"Those who are benevolent toward others love people." These words by Confucius summarize his highest evaluation of "benevolence." To put "love of people" into practice, one must in a negative sense strive to "save others from what one wishes to avoid oneself" and, in a positive sense, "help others if you want to help yourself."

We can hardly say that "benevolence" is not needed in our time and in our society.

Red Guard comment:

The relationships between slaveowners and slaves, between landlords and peasants, and between capitalists and workers are those of exploiters and the exploited. The struggle between them is a life-and-death struggle—totally devoid of the idea of "loving one another" and "embracing one another." In a Socialist society in which classes and class struggle still exist, the primary reason why these monsters and demons have openly propagated the idea of "loving and embracing one another" is to blur the class boundary line and to repudiate class struggle.

"A Christian Village"*

Korean communities have existed in north China for many generations. They are Chinese citizens and in most ways have adopted Chinese culture. This is a story of one of those communities. Similar stories have been published about Chinese Christian groups.

I am eighteen years old. My parents, foster parents actually, have asked me to tell you about our church and our community. Not because they don't want to do it themselves but because they feel my Mandarin is better than theirs. Also, I have been with the church since I was two years old and I know it quite well. We are a small Korean minority community of about eighty families. There is a much larger one some fifty kilometers away with over 400 families. In our case, we are all Christian. The heads of the households make a solemn pledge every year at Easter that our whole village will live forever in devotion to our Lord Jesus Christ. Then it is the young people's turn. Last year, the weather was freezing. Nevertheless, we had our traditional Easter outdoor service early in the morning. It was still dark; I could not count the number of people there. We could not sing at all; it was too cold. We raised high our arms and prayed, received special blessings from the elders, and returned to our homes.

Pastor John Tsai has been our pastor for many years. He's been with us right from the beginning. For the past three years, however, he has not been able to leave his house, so he blesses the buns and the wine, and the deacons carry them into the church, and we have the fellowship of the holy communion. We have fixed a loudspeaker in his room so he can follow the service. We have a big room across the open courtyard, capable of seating sixty people along the four walls. Other people bring small wooden stools, so we can seat about 120 altogether in three rows all around. We have been thinking of putting in benches, but wood is difficult to come by.

My real father's family name is Tsou. He was a welder. When I was two, he was killed in an accident. My mother, whom I can hardly remember now, wanted very much to go home to her relatives in Korea. But then she probably had to make a child bride of me, otherwise who would want to spend money to feed another family's girl? She did not want to do this. Then my foster parents came along and offered to bring me up, provided I took their name. They had no child of their own. And their wanting me to carry their name guaranteed that I would not be made a child bride. So my mother agreed and went home. She did not write back. A few years later word came through that she had married, and wanted me to be obedient to my foster parents.

My foster parents are very kind people. Both are deeply pious Christians. As an elder, my father is one of the leaders of the church and of the community. One of his tasks is to see to it that parents bring up their children in the Christian way. He is so conscientious that at one

*From *Households of God on China's Soil* by Raymond Fung, Orbis Books, Maryknoll, New York, 1983.

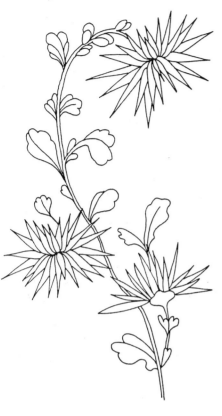

time he had a class at home for young parents on Christian parenthood. He still takes special pains to call in the young people one by one to have long talks with them. His other regular task is the morning prayer at 6:30 every day for some twenty families in the neighbourhood. Normally four or five show up, sometimes ten. I did not attend until I was fifteen. After I was fifteen, I grew up much quicker. I became aware of the problems of the church and of my neighbours. My father is a very different person when he is praying. Normally he is very strict, and capable. People come to him for all kinds of advice. But when praying, he is much gentler, and he does not scold people.

My father told me specifically to tell our evangelism story. Eight or nine years ago, our village was not all Christian. My blood mother was not a Christian. We had a lot of problems among us. Some wives are of Korean blood, some Han. One of the problems, I understand, had to do with coke [coal]. We depend on coke for fuel to keep our room warm. It so happened that the Korean women felt that the Han women were getting better quality coke, in bigger pieces and at the same price, thanks to their family ties with those in charge. This was the beginning. Soon the men were drawn in. It was bad. People did not talk to each other.

The crisis came during an extremely cold winter. A baby boy died in the night. The mother almost went crazy. She made wild accusations regarding the quality of the coke and why it went dead in the middle of the night. Things became very tense. The heads of the families came together to deal with the accusation and find a solution to the matter of coke distribution. There were Christians on both sides. For some time, the discussion got nowhere. Then Brother Lee, whose wife is Han, volunteered to share his coke with others. Nobody took him seriously. But he did what he promised. After work hours, he would bring a few kilos of coke and give it to a Korean family. Nobody knew what game he was playing. He simply walked in, gave his greetings and said: "I've come to see if you need coke. This is fine coke." If there was no response, he would simply leave the coke by the stove and go away. Sometimes they would examine the coke, chat about its quality and have tea. One Sunday, after the service, Elder Chong asked Brother Lee to come up. He embraced him in front of everybody, and told the church what Brother Lee had done. He said: "Brother Lee alone acted like our Lord. He showed us the way." Brother Lee was moved to tears. Elder Chong could not contain himself either. Soon everybody was crying and confessing their sins to each other.

Some time later, the heads of the families came together to continue their negotiations. My father said that about two-thirds were not Christians then. At the meeting, the Christians from both sides offered to share their coke, not just once but always. It broke the stalemate. Within a year, according to my father, all the family heads became Christian and were baptized. And they took their wives and children into the church as well. This was how ours became a Christian village.

Evangelism is very important for us. Father insists that it must begin with the heads of families; otherwise, he reasons, what right does he have to be the family head? So he puts in a lot of effort as an elder to get parents to be good Christians and to teach their wives and children about God. When it's his turn to preach, he likes to ask the people to commit themselves to preaching the gospel to their neighbours. He would ask people to raise their hands. He would have a young man take down their names. Later in the week, or the next Sunday, he would get hold of these people one by one and ask them how they were faring.

Meeting of the Three Clowns*

This short, didactic drama makes fun of old-style religious and superstitious practices while praising the commonsense attitudes of revolutionary youth.

Kuanyin: the goddess of mercy.

It is spring in a North China village. Mother Chao comes to light incense before the Kuanyin shrine. She has been busy for days and has not had time to come. She thinks that this is why her small grandson has caught a fever.

Suddenly Hsiu-yu, her daughter, comes upon her and blows out the match with which her mother is about to light the incense.

Hsiu-yu sings:

> *The clay Buddha statue only knows how to deceive people.*
> *Lighting incense and kowtowing is making trouble for yourself.*
> *How many times have I told you*
> *To break off all relations with that thing!*
> *We are an army family and I am a cadre.*
> *We should take the lead in destroying superstition.*
> *Trees have roots and water has a source.*
> *The only way to cure sickness is to call a doctor.*

cadre: a local government official.

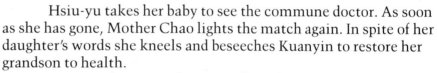

Hsiu-yu takes her baby to see the commune doctor. As soon as she has gone, Mother Chao lights the match again. In spite of her daughter's words she kneels and beseeches Kuanyin to restore her grandson to health.

Ironmouth Sun is a fortune-teller who has fallen on hard days since the Communists came, but there are still a few families that believe in his magic. He has heard that Mother Chao's grandson is ill and so he comes to see her, hoping to badger some of her food tickets. He is rather hesitant because he fears Hsiu-yu, who has exposed him at a commune meeting as a "blowfly spreading superstition."

Sun tells Mother Chao that the doctor will not be able to cure the child. He asks for money to offer to the "heaven-master" so that he can find out what will happen. When Mother Chao gives him the money, he says that she must take the child out forty-nine steps in an eastward direction the following morning, to remove him from the influence of the evil star that is causing his illness. Mother Chao thanks him and asks him to continue to worship the "heaven-master" on her behalf. Sun says that he is afraid that the "heaven-master" will not stay with him much longer as he has nothing to give him to eat. Mother Chao then goes to fetch some rice for him.

While Mother Chao is away, Third Auntie Chien arrives. She often pretends to be a medium for a spirit in order to get more money for clothes and cigarettes. Afraid of meeting Hsiu-yu, she first calls out

*By Liu Hou-ming in *China's Youth*, December 14, 1963, in *Religious Policy and Practice in Communist China* by Donald MacInnis, Macmillan and Co., 1972.

geomancy: the pseudo-science of locating a building site.

for her from the gate. Should Hsiu-yu be at home she will say that she wants to be given some work for the commune.

Sun, sipping tea, hears someone calling out "Hsiu-yu, Hsiu-yu!" and is terrified. He hides under the table. When Mother Chao comes back with a bag of rice, Sun is nowhere to be seen. She goes to answer the gate. Third Auntie Chien asks if the tea is poured out for her. "Why, yes," replies Mother Chao politely, "your spirit came before you."

At once Third Auntie Chien starts to shake and cry out. Mother Chao hurriedly kneels down and welcomes the spirit. Auntie Chien talks in half-riddles, saying that the spirit needs "three feet of red cloth and two of blue, a pig and a bottle of wine" before the baby can be freed from the ghost that possesses it. She also demands money and the bag of rice lying on the table. Ironmouth Sun mutters furiously from under the table but dares not show himself. Auntie Chien takes the incense from in front of Kuanyin and gives it to Mother Chao as a medicine. Finally she recovers from her fit and pretends to ask what happened. She demands money from Mother Chao and drags her off to open the money-chest.

Hu Yinyang comes by the house and notices a new barn built alongside. Hu specialized in geomancy before the liberation. Now he decides to tell Mother Chao that her baby's illness is due to the position of the barn.

Third Auntie Chien hears someone at the gate and decides that she had better hide under the table. She bumps into Ironmouth Sun. They have no time to argue over the bag of rice but both crouch under the tablecloth. Mother Chao lets Hu in and he immediately says that the barn must be pulled down. He offers to read from his book on geomancy if she will give him five dollars. Mother Chao confesses that she does not know what to do, as she has been given so much different advice.

Hu Yinyang starts to call Sun and Third Auntie Chien names, and then stops suddenly. He sees the table moving as though inspired by a host. The other two "clowns" emerge and wrangle with each other over the best advice and who should have the bag of rice. Auntie Chien sings:

Yinyang Hu, the old tomcat,
It's bad luck for a house when he goes there!
Longlegs Wang got his son a wife
And built a beautiful three-roomed house to the north.
Then Yinyang Hu did some divining
And insisted that the new house be pulled down for the
*   sake of the couple's future.*
Longlegs listened to Yinyang Hu
And pulled down the three-roomed house in a hurry.
The young bride was furious when she heard it
And said that a superstitious household was no good!
Hu Yinyang, the old tomcat;

> *Ruined the three-roomed house*
> *And spoilt a romance!*
> *Never believe him.*
> *I am better than he is!*

Ironmouth Sun sings:

> *Third Auntie Chien's belly is full of ghosts*
> *Fighting to give incense ash to the sick!*
> *Widow Wang in our village sprained her leg when she went out*
> *And she gave her incense ash to eat!*
> *She ate three packets with no result*
> *And still hobbles about with a stick.*
> *Neither of them are any good,*
> *You had better believe in me!*

Hu Yinyang sings:

> *Ironmouth Sun is a greedyguts*
> *And all he knows about fortune telling*
> *Is 'Spirit-star in the West, go to the West,*
> *Spirit-star in the East, go to the East,'*
> *If you do as he says*
> *It will be the death of your grandson!*
> *I know more than any of them,*
> *And you must do as I say!*

Auntie Chien is on the point of throwing another fit when Hsiu-yu arrives with the child. His temperature has gone since the doctor gave him penicillin. Mother Chao asks the three whether she should still follow their advice and they hurriedly withdraw it. Hisu-yu then recalls their hard life before the liberation and explains that talk about "fate" was meant to stop poor people like them from rising against the landlords. Mother Chao sees how useless and wasteful superstition is, and turns over the incense pot and the Kuanyin statue. Mother Chao and Hsiu-yu sing:

> *Many old ways of thought have been left by the old society and*
> *the old systems,*
> *Only when the old ways of thought have been torn out by the*
> *roots can we be really liberated.*
> *Do not believe in spirits or ghosts; down with all fuedal*
> *superstitions!*
> *Burn up old ways of thought and old customs like paper boats*
> *and lanterns!*
> *Obey the voice of Chairman Mao,*
> *Look ahead when you walk,*
> *Resolve to do away with the old and set up the new,*
> *And always follow the government and Party!*

Hsiu-yu then takes the three "clowns" to the production brigade for punishment.

Excerpts from *The Song of Ouyang Hai*

The Song of Ouyang Hai* commemmorates the life of Ouyang Hai, age 23, a squad leader in the army who died while pushing a horse loaded with ammunition out of the path of a train, saving the train loaded with his comrades. The following are excerpts of this widely-read story:

Hai charged on to the tracks and, with all his might, pushed the horse out of the path of the train.

The train was not derailed, the passengers were saved, Hai's companions by the roadside were saved, state property was saved, a tragedy was averted. But Comrade Ouyang Hai was crushed beneath the massive train wheels. He lay in a pool of blood.

"Squad leader...." His comrades flew to him with a heart-broken cry. The pass threw back a mournful echo. The Hsiang River water, the surrounding mountains, responded sorrowfully:

"Ouyang Hai...."

Hai lay in his comrades' arms. His eyes were open and clear, and he looked calmly at the undamaged train, at the passengers safe and sound, at the Hsiang River flowing north, at the sky from which a fine drizzle was falling. In the distance were majestic peaks. Nearby the white pagoda stood proudly on the hilltop.

The train rushed the badly hurt Hai to the county seat, where a waiting ambulance sped with him to a hospital.

With tears in their eyes, people softly called his name. Hundreds of soldiers and passengers from the train rolled up their sleeves and offered blood....

Hai lay quietly on his bed, the blood of class brothers flowing into his body, slowly, drop by drop, through a transfusion tube. He was so calm, so peaceful. On his face there was no trace of pain. It was as if he had just returned from completing some task and was smilingly thinking of taking up another and heavier load for socialist construction.

Suddenly, the flow of blood through the tube ceased. Hai's heart had stopped beating. His eyes slowly closed. A short and glorious life of twenty-three years had come to an end.

*From the editorial, "Emulate Wang Chieh, Great Revolutionary Fighter," *Peking Review*, November 12, 1965.

Do Not Spit at Random—A One-Act Play by Fang Tzu

This street play, which has been performed many times on the street corners of Hangzhou and Shanghai, was written by the Hangzhou Stage Group in support of the patriotic health movement. It is typical of the purpose which undergirds almost all contemporary writing in China, and it stresses in particular the vigilance of the Young Pioneers, children of nine to thirteen years.

(A young girl Pioneer with a megaphone comes out from a crowd in the street, or from among the audience in a theater.)

YOUNG PIONEER: Dear uncles and aunts, please do not spit at random. Spitting at random on the ground is a most deplorable habit. It helps to spread germs and disease, and so may affect our health harmfully. Dear uncles and aunts, if you want to spit, please do so in a cuspidor. If there is no cuspidor at hand, then spit into a handkerchief.

PASSER-BY (walks across stage with a briefcase, makes noise as if going to spit): Hmmm...hawk...choo! (Spits phlegm on the ground.)

YOUNG PIONEER (seeing the passer-by spit, hurries away from the crowd to overtake the man, or leaps onto stage from below): Uncle, uncle, don't spit on the ground. Please rub it away with a piece of paper.

PASSER-BY: My young friend, with the cuspidor so far away, where do you think I should spit?

YOUNG PIONEER: You can go up to the cuspidor. It's only a few steps away.

PASSER-BY: I'd have to go there and come back again. How do you think I am going to catch my bus?

YOUNG PIONEER: Uncle, don't you know there are many germs in spittle? When it dries, the germs will be scattered everywhere, and, by breathing the air, people may be infected with such diseases as typhoid, diptheria, tuberculosis.

PASSER-BY: I don't have tuberculosis! So there cannot be any germs in the phlegm I coughed out.

YOUNG PIONEER: It is a social obligation to refrain from spitting at random. If everyone spits and insists that there can be no germs in what he has spat, how can we be patriotic and keep ourselves in good health?

ONE OF THE CROWD (speaks from the crowd or from the audience in a theater): Rub the spit away quickly. (A large crowd gathers around the passer-by.)

PASSER-BY (irritated): Hmm. You want me to squat there and rub away the spit? But I have no time for that. Besides, I am not used to doing that sort of thing. (Prepares to go.)

YOUNG PIONEER: Uncle, Uncle, don't go. I haven't finished with you yet.

PASSER-BY: I have to go home now to my dinner and have no time to carry on a conversation with you.

ONE OF THE CROWD: Hey, you come back here! There can't be a more unreasonable man than you.

PASSER-BY: How so?

YOUNG PIONEER (offering a piece of paper): Uncle, please rub it away with this piece of paper.

PASSER-BY: I won't do it.

YOUNG PIONEER: How can you refuse to carry out a social obligation?

PASSER-BY: Are you lecturing me?

(Here a number of actors come out of the crowd to speak, or speak from among the audience, or some may go up on the stage.)

CROWD: What? You are trying to put on airs? Don't argue with him. Call the police. Police! Comrade Police!

PASSER-BY: I won't rub it. I promise not to spit again.

CROWD: Comrade, what is your work unit?

PASSER-BY: That's none of your business.

CROWD: Why isn't it my business? When you refuse to carry out a public obligation, everyone is entitled to criticize you.

PEOPLE'S POLICE (enters): What's happened here? (At this moment the crowd becomes larger.)

CROWD: He spat on the sidewalk and refuses to accept criticism. He would not listen to a child's advice. And he's such a big man. He is no better than this child. And he is a Party member too! Probably a backward one.

PEOPLE'S POLICE: All right, it's clear to me now. (Addressing the crowd): Comrades! What do you think we should do with such a man?

CROWD: He should be criticized and fined. He should be made the subject of a wall newspaper. A cartoon should be drawn of him for all to see. He should be taken to the police station.

PEOPLE'S POLICE: Oh, well, if you will not rub it away, I'll do it for you. But, first of all, may I know what unit you belong to?

PASSER-BY: As for that—

(The voice of a middle-aged woman is heard off-stage calling someone.)

MOTHER: Shao-ying, Shao-ying.

YOUNG PIONEER: Oh, Mama!

MOTHER: There you are. We've been waiting for you a long time. The meal is cold. Won't you hurry home to your meal?

YOUNG PIONEER: I haven't finished my work yet.

MOTHER: Work? What sort of work?

YOUNG PIONEER: Someone has spat on the ground and refuses to accept criticism. Unless he cleans it off, I am not going to let him go.

MOTHER (recognized the passer-by): Oh, is that you, Comrade Ch'en?

PASSER-BY: Er—yes, it's me, Teacher Wang.

MOTHER: Shao-ying, who is it that refuses to accept criticism?

YOUNG PIONEER: Mama, there he is.

PEOPLE'S POLICE (addressing mother): Comrade, do you know which unit this comrade belongs to?

MOTHER: He is the accountant of the cotton mill. He is Comrade Ch'en Jung-fa.

PEOPLE'S POLICE: Good, thank you. (Addressing the passer-by): I think there's only one way now.

(Draws a circle around the spittle on the ground with a piece of chalk, and is about to write down the name of the passer-by and the unit to which he belongs.)

PASSER-BY (frightened): Comrade, don't! Don't write down the name of my unit! (Addressing the crowd): Comrades and my young friend, please pardon me this once. You may write my name there, but please do not write the name of our mill too. Our mill has already signed a patriotic health agreement.

PEOPLE'S POLICE: Yet you break the agreement?

PASSER-BY: All right, I'll clean it, I'll clean it. I promise not to do the same thing again.

YOUNG PIONEER: Here, take this piece of paper.

(The passer-by squats down to rub the ground. Crowd, satisfied, disperses.)

PEOPLE'S POLICE (to mother): Comrade, your child is really a good Young Pioneer, a young heroine for the elimination of the seven pests (mosquitoes, flies, rats, sparrows, and so forth) and for public health. If everyone eliminates the seven pests in earnest and maintains public hygiene as she does, our cities and the countryside will be rid of the seven pests sooner, disease will largely be wiped out, people will be healthier than ever, and the nation will be more prosperous and stronger.

MOTHER: Shao-ying, hurry home to your meal. It's already cold.

YOUNG PIONEER: Mama, my group leader isn't here yet. I'll go home when he comes to relieve me.

MOTHER: Oh, well, I'll have to warm the meal again anyway.

YOUNG PIONEER (speaking through megaphone and coming toward crowd in the street or toward audience in theater): Dear uncles and aunts, please do not spit at random. Spitting at random is a most deplorable habit....

The "Most Admired Persons" Poll

A ballot for the "Most Admired Men" and "Most Admired Women" Poll appears annually in the September issue of Good Housekeeping *magazine.* Readers send in their ballots, ranking their first, second, and third choices, and give the reasons for their selections. Here are the top ten winners for 1987. Note the range, from religious leaders to politicians to actors and actresses.*

The Most Admired Women

1. Mother Teresa of Calcutta, 11th year in top 10.
2. First Lady Nancy Reagan, hailed for her leadership in the war against drugs, was in first place last year.
3. Philippines President Corazon Aquino, up from the fourth spot in 1986.
4. Oprah Winfrey, actress and TV talk show hostess, first appearance on the list.
5. British Prime Minister Margaret Thatcher, up from seventh spot last year.
6. Pat Nixon, wife of ex-President Richard Nixon, 18th year in top 10; was number eight last year.
7. Phyllis Schlafly, advocate of women's role in the home, was number three last year.
8. Betty Ford, wife of former President Gerald Ford.
9. Jeane Kirkpatrick, former U.S. ambassador to the United Nations.
10. Katharine Hepburn, long-time favorite actress, was number six last year.

The Most Admired Men

1. President Ronald Reagan, seventh year as number one.
2. Reverend Billy Graham, seventh year in top 10; was number three last year.
3. Bill Cosby, star of hit TV comedy show, third year in top 10; was number five last year.
4. Pope John Paul II, same spot as last year.
5. Bob Hope, actor, seventh year in top 10; was number eight last year.
6. Lee Iacocca, president of Chrysler Corporation, sixth year in top 10; same spot as last year.
7. Former President Jimmy Carter, third year in top ten, up from number 10 last year.
8. Tom Selleck, actor, reappears in the top 10 this year.
9. Reverend Norman Vincent Peale, was number 10 in 1985.
10. Lech Walesa, leader of the Solidarity movement in Poland, a reappearance; was number six in 1985.

*From *Good Housekeeping*, January, 1988.

Here are some reasons that readers gave for their choices:

For the men, most frequently cited were qualities of courage, faith, honesty, leadership, patriotism, talent, dedication, helpfulness to others, and upholding family values.

For the women, Mother Teresa's strong supporters made comments like this: "I admire her total commitment to helping the poor and needy," and "She is a saint in our times." Other readers based their choices on such values as courage, selflessness, faith, compassion, personal integrity, strong family values, career accomplishment, poise, and setting a good example for the younger generation.

Mediation Settles a Divorce Case*

Zhang married Wang in 1964, and they had a boy and a girl. They often quarrelled because they were of different temperaments. In 1979, Zhang became acquainted with a married woman, and their frequent contacts led to more serious quarrels between husband and wife. Finally, they lived separately. In 1982, Zhang brought a suit to the court for a divorce. Wang disagreed and charged him with "abandoning his wife for loving the new and loathing the old," and asked the court for fair treatment.

After the case was accepted by the court, both parties appointed a lawyer. Instead of pursuing the individual interests of their clients in court, the lawyers worked together and tried to reason with the two parties.

Both lawyers agreed that Zhang and Wang got married voluntarily, but the marriage was not well-founded. They did not really have deep feelings for each other, and their relationship gradually deteriorated because of endless quarrels. Although the primary reason for divorce was Zhang's change of heart, the two had not lived together in harmony for a long time. It was likely their conflicts would worsen.

The case had two possible outcomes—reconciliation or divorce. Although there was little hope of reunion, the lawyers tried their utmost to mediate. If their attempt for a reunion failed, they would continue mediation for a divorce.

The court and Zhang's lawyer first tried to reason with the husband. During mediation, they tactfully pointed out his shortcomings and mistakes, and stated the possibilities for reconciliation should he decide to change his mind. They suggested he consider his son and daughter, who were not yet adults, and the feelings of his wife, who had been with him for nearly twenty years. The judge and the lawyer even took time to visit Zhang personally.

The court and Wang's lawyer also talked to her, encouraging her to take the initiative to be on good terms with her husband.

Both sides were touched by the consideration of the judges and the lawyers. Zhang admitted his mistakes, and Wang acknowledged her shortcomings. But, as there were still deep differences between their temperaments, they could not agree to reunite. However, the two became less antagonistic and were able to sit down and talk.

The lawyers then began to mediate for a divorce. They mainly spoke with Wang, asking her to consider the condition of her marriage. Even if the court decided on reconciliation, the conflicts would continue and there would be no happiness in the family. She finally came to understand that by opposing the divorce she was only prolonging her suffering.

*From *Beijing Review*, February 13, 1984.

Once Wang agreed to the divorce, everything was settled smoothly, including who would look after the children and the division of property. Zhang made some concessions to express his gratitude to the court and the lawyers. Both children stayed with their mother, so he gave Wang some money and bought her a television set.

The case was settled to the satisfaction of both the husband and wife. They thanked the judges and lawyers for their kindness and consideration.

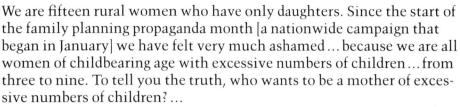

Life Without a Son*

We are fifteen rural women who have only daughters. Since the start of the family planning propaganda month [a nationwide campaign that began in January] we have felt very much ashamed...because we are all women of childbearing age with excessive numbers of children...from three to nine. To tell you the truth, who wants to be a mother of excessive numbers of children?...

Yet the fifteen of us are not ready to give up. Even if we had to die, we would still want to try to have a son so that we might be able to hold our heads up.

Why do we want to risk our lives to do this painful thing—to hurt our country and ourselves? It is because here, where we are, a mother without a son suffers so much discrimination and cruelty that it is worth risking our lives to escape it.

Let us give you a few examples and you will understand how much we have suffered:

When there is a wedding in the village, a mother with a son is invited to prepare the bed for the newlyweds. She is called the "perfect person." We who have no sons are forbidden to touch anything on the bed, and when the bride enters the house, we are ordered to stay at a distance. The people call us nuisances.

We, the nuisances, suffer bullying from our husbands and insults from our in-laws. Even our own parents sometimes blame us for not bringing them honor.

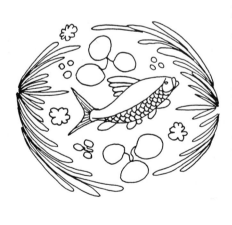

When we are out in public, the situation is even worse. We dare not demand fairness, and we dare not question things that seem to us improper....

Recently, the wife of a village cadre gave birth to a son after four daughters. They had a feast and distributed a lot of eggs. The husband was full of smiles and the in-laws were overjoyed....However, one year later, this same woman gave birth to another girl. The husband did not go into the room to see her, and the in-laws cursed her....Now, her personal status has dropped a hundredfold....

We...ask the state...to adopt a law stipulating that whoever publicizes the view of preferring men over women, and whoever insults mothers who only have daughters, be punished by law. Furthermore, the law should be posted in large characters on the walls of the rural areas to be printed deeply into the hearts of the people. The momentum must be as great as that when we obtained our first liberation....

*From *China's One-Child Families: Girls Need Not Apply,* by Lynn Landman. Translated from *People's Daily,* Feb. 23, 1983.

Between the Older and Younger Generations*

Retired worker Luo Jiuzhang and his wife live with their 40-year-old only son and daughter-in-law because housing shortages prevented the younger couple from moving to their own home after their marriage.

Luo's daughter-in-law, the eldest girl of a well-to-do family, was not good at doing housework. Her mother-in-law was not satisfied with her, and she thought the old lady was too garrulous. They often quarrelled, and their relationship gradually became strained.

Finally, the two generations began to cook and eat their meals separately. When the older couple fell ill, the younger couple did not care for them.

At the beginning of the "five goods" family campaign, the neighbourhood committee, a self-administering grassroots organization, publicized the significance of the campaign and the "five goods" criteria at meetings and on public blackboards. Then, the residents elected the first group of "five goods" families. This served as an incentive for the other 10,000 Chenjiaqiao households to emulate these examples.

Under these circumstances, the inharmonious Luo family became a problem. Their neighbours, as well as cadres at the neighbourhood committee often visited them, trying to persuade them to mend their ways. The Luo family members were moved by their neighbours' concern. They began to forgive and help each other and the tensions relaxed. The daughter-in-law, who used to address her parents-in-law with "hey," began calling them "father" and "mother."

Today the family has changed. When the elders fall ill, their daughter-in-law accompanies them to the hospital and prepares medicinal herbs and food for them. She also asks her children to help with their grandparents' housework and invites them to watch TV in her room. There are no longer quarrels in the Luo family, according to their neighbours.

Not long ago the Luo family was selected a "five goods" family. But the daughter-in-law said they did not deserve it. "We have made some progress," she noted, "but ours is not yet as harmonious as other 'five goods' families."

The experience of the Chenjiaqiao neighbourhood shows that it is not easy to obtain the campaign's main goals: Let all people love one another; let all families be harmonious. However, the "five goods" family campaign has already achieved good results and it has promoted social morality. In Huayuangang, a section of the Chenjiaqiao neighbourhood, the monthly average of civil disputes has decreased from seven to one and in 1982 its larceny cases were cut by half, compared with the previous year.

*From *Beijing Review*, July 18, 1983.

LETTERS FROM CHINESE YOUTH

The following are excerpts from a few of the thousands of letters that were sent to the editor of Chinese Youth *in response to Pan Xiao's anguished letter.* In contrast to the usual upbeat style of articles supporting official policy, the editor printed a broad range of letters, many of them critical or opposed to the offical Party or government line. Here is an authentic window into the hearts of Chinese youth today.*

Letters of Sympathy and Encouragement

Many of the letter-writers sent gifts of money or writing paper to help Pan Xiao (an aspiring writer) to pursue her chosen vocation. Others comforted and encouraged her by describing their own victory over bitter experiences, assuring her that she, too, could rise above misfortune and discouragement.

From a Youth in Xinxiang, Henan Province:

> *For the first time I heard from someone else the song of my own heart. Though filled with tears and flames, the song sings the true feelings of my heart!...I send you six yuan. Just use it for some writing paper. You must accept it.*

From Six Youths in Wuhan:

Six youths from Wuhan sent a parcel containing a plastic miniature plum tree, an elegantly decorated diary book, and a heap of envelopes and letter paper. On the front page of the diary, and also in their letter, they wrote:

> *Pan Xiao, when you put your letter in the mailbox, did you think that it was merely a slip of paper? No, it has already become tinder. It has rekindled the almost dying fire of life of young people like us. Let us join our hands in future studies and exploration. Let us look reality in the face and open a road leading to the ideal state!*

From Zheng Yi, Yuci, Shanxi Province:

> *Comrade little Pan, it is my feeling that you have not truly seen through life. For thousands of years humans have been tenaciously in search of the value of existence; they seek the truth of life, pursuing the true, the good, and the beautiful. You are only twenty-three years old, and your experience cannot be regarded*

* From ''What Is the Meaning of Life?'', selections from *Chinese Youth* (Zhongguo Qingnian), in *Chinese Education*, Armonk, NY: M. E. Sharpe, 1981.

as profound and mature. It is inappropriate for you to blurt out the two words "see through." Your understanding at this stage is only one phase of your life. You will not stop at this point, and your path is by no means narrowing. Precisely because you are persistently exploring and are not fearful of hardships, you are standing at the threshold of truth. It is possible for you to find a valuable life, and thus become a most enthusiastic and valiant fighter. Of course, we cannot rule out the other possibility. Don't hide yourself in romantic love, and don't evade the crisis of your faith, but move forward to meet it head-on. Your age is the best time to solve the problem of your outlook on life. If you turn from it, you will achieve nothing in your whole life; if you step up to it and find a good solution, you will sweep forward irresistibly like water pouring from a steep pool.

From Jin Yi, Beijing:

One should be good at exploring people's hearts, be good at understanding others deeply. In life you will see no end of things that are false, evil and ugly, but here are also the true, the good, and the beautiful that are even more numerous and are too numerous to be counted. In your own experience of life, didn't you get your close schoolmates' help in your adversity, and win the sincere sympathy of cadres in the subdistrict office?

From Zhou Rumao, Macheng, Hubei:

How should we walk along the path of life: what do we struggle for? What should we do if we run into snags?

Life must have an ideal, and idealism is the twin of struggle. Human life is like this: on the one hand, it is filled with light, hope, and joy; on the other hand, it may yield darkness, evil, and pain. There are years when the weather is favorable, and there are times when natural and man-made calamities prevail. You may have smooth sailing success, but you may also suffer setbacks and defeats. To live is to overcome difficulties, sweep away obstacles, and propel society forward. One should remedy what is irrational, create more wealth for society, and open up a renewed and more plentiful life.

From Zheng Deping, Chuxian, Anhui

To begin life is like learning to ride a bicycle. Both your and my experiences show that we tripped and fell, like falling off bicycles. When learning to ride a bicycle, we have the spirit of trying again after we fall off. Why don't we learn how to lead a life in the spirit of learning to ride a bicycle?

Letters Supporting a Life Style of Unselfish Service

Many of the letter-writers, despite unhappy experiences, had not given up their idealism and their commitment to the goals of "serve the people" and "fight selfishness." They recognize the need to earn a living, and to take care of the ordinary daily needs of a person. But, they say, there also are spiritual needs that can only be satisfied by making contributions to the welfare of other people and the nation. Only by devoting our lives to others, as well as to ourselves, can we achieve our full human potential.

From Zhu Peifen, Zhang Qu, Guilin:

Aside from material goods needed for the sustenance of life, people also need a rich and colorful spiritual and cultural life (including such things as ideals, ambition, dedication, honor, etc.). Needs of these two kinds comprise man's total needs. The former needs are the most essential, but of a lower grade. The latter are not essential, but of a higher grade; they are one of the major reasons for the evolution of human society, from a lower and uncouth stage to a higher civilization.

From Pu Lin, Guangxi:

We should admit that there is indeed a selfish side to man's character, just as we should admit that there is an ugly side to life. But we must also admit that there are noble-minded people, and the number is not few. Of course, what they see and what they do may sometimes relate to their own concerns, either consciously or unconsciously. But I do not think we can describe this as "selfishness" in very general terms.... For the interests of the people, many have ventured their lives. It is precisely at a moment of life and death that they faithfully "abide by the lofty ethics and ideas," as Comrade Pan Xiao suggested.

From Zhu Jiaming, a Student in Shanghai:

... To strive for one's own existence is not selfish; nor is it selfish to be busy running about to make a living. Only when one tries to further one's own interests at the expense of others, can it be seen as despicable and ugly selfishness. How can it be called a "selfish desire" if one wants to live a better life? Some of my schoolmates, friends, and I do not cherish the noble idea of "living to make others live even better"; nevertheless, we all have the desire to make more contributions to society, the motherland, the people as long as we are alive.

Letters that say "Serve Yourself First"

A surprising number of writers rejected the official values and said that a person's first responsibility is to seek personal happiness and career goals. There is a strong note of cynicism in these letters. They speak of "human nature," and the need for economic incentives to achieve the "Four Modernizations." As for the hero models, like Lei Feng (a young soldier who gave his life for his comrades), one writer asks, "How many Lei Fengs are there in real life?"

From a High School Student in Shanghai:

As I see it, the path of life means money, position, and personal happiness. This differs entirely from what I used to think and say: that one lives for the happiness, interests, and needs of others. In the real society at present, everything is decided by money, position, and personal happiness.

From Fu Jiangnan, Nanchang, Jiangxi Province:

To make a living in real life, one must first of all make every effort to meet one's own needs, and then the needs of other people. This is the law of human nature. It is just like the Yellow River, which became the cradle of the Chinese nation, because the river itself has abundant water resources and strong vitality. For one's self—this is the most primitive motive for man's thinking and consciousness; it cannot be destroyed or created by anyone.

From Pu Wu, Nanjing, Jiangsu Province:

I quite approve and appreciate Comrade Pan Xiao's opinions regarding the meaning of life. I, too, hold that people in today's society live for their own interests. Without individual incentive, people would be like a car out of fuel: it cannot be started. Some people may have this to say: "Didn't Comrade Lei Feng live all his life selflessly, and because of this earn the respect of all?" To this question I can only answer: "True, Comrade Lei Feng was respectable. But how many Lei Fengs are there in real life? I have never seen anyone half as good as Lei Feng, much less people of the Lei Feng type."

From Wei Qiang, Zigong, Sichuan Province:

Many viewpoints contained in Pan Xiao's letter are the same as mine. Words such as "modernization endeavor," "dedicating one's life to the emancipation of all mankind" are all lies. Right now, how many young people are there working with all their

energy in the factories, and how many youths are there who study arduously for the sake of revolution! In a word, if they do not work for a bonus or study for their own future, what else do they work or study for! Fulfilling the four modernizations program is our common ideal. But ideal is not "reality"; reality is disappointing everywhere.

Letters Referring to Social Problems

Some writers referred to social problems that contradicted the official policies and values—"brave words and exciting slogans" which in the end are but "empty political theories." A teacher refers to the problem of the "back door"—meaning the use of personal connections by government and Party officials to get special favors for themselves and their children.

From Xie Xie, Jiangyu, Sichuan Province:

Comrade editors, when publishing the letter, did you realize that it refers to a serious social problem at present that can neither be denied nor evaded! Discussion on the meaning of life is necessary. But I have doubts about what will come out of it. Perhaps the result will again be: brave words, exciting slogans, firm determinations, superb but empty political theories, etc. If they were to be compared with the fact that "three plus two makes five," a fact that everybody recognizes and accepts, which of the two would endure!

From Yao Zonglie, a Teacher in Jinan, Shandong Province:

True, the feelings of youth about a "spiritual crisis" and a "crisis of survival" are related to the ten years of calamity [the Cultural Revolution] brought about by Lin Biao and the "Gang of Four." But at present, the most important cause for this is the influence of social ills. At schools, we teachers educate students to study hard and embrace a revolutionary outlook on life. But when returning home or coming into contact with society, the students find that some of their schoolmates get good jobs through special connections (the "back door"), and lead a good life even though they are "of poor character and scholarship." In such cases, all our painstaking and well-intentioned preaching becomes futile. Isn't this a heavy blow to the students who are "of good character and scholarship!"

Letters Mentioning Duty to the Nation

By and large, there is very little reference to patriotism and political ideology in these letters. The two excerpts that follow speak of the interrelationship among the interest of the individual, the motherland, and the people.

From Bei Yiran, Harbin, Heilongjiang Province:

> *Discussing the meaning of life today is not merely a question of how we should view life; it is an issue involving how the state (nation) should handle the relationship between the interests of individuals, and those of the collective; that is, whether proper personal interests, that do not encroach upon the interests of others, can be recognized and respected by society.*

From Che Guocheng, Dalian, Liaoning Province:

> *If we compare life to a big river, it is formed by the convergence of all tributaries, including oneself, the motherland, and the people. "For oneself" is one of the sources, but by no means the only one.*

Guide to Resources

The Guide to Resources section contains supplementary resource materials that can be obtained for use in conjunction with *Focus On China*. It lists periodicals and teacher's guides, books on China, primary sources from China, audio-visual guides and resources, as well as national/regional resource centers on China and Asia that offer programs and resource assistance to secondary school curriculums.

PERIODICALS AND TEACHERS' GUIDES

Focus on Asian Studies, a quarterly published by the Asia Society (725 Park Avenue, New York, NY 10021), is the best periodical on China and Asia for teachers. Each issue is devoted to a special theme, with articles, class activities, book reviews and listings of resources and curriculum guides.

China, A Teaching Workbook (East Asian Curriculum Project, East Asian Institute, Columbia University, 420 W. 118 Street, New York, NY 10027), is the most comprehensive collection of curriculum materials and resource guides. This looseleaf volume is organized into fourteen sections ranging from Art, to U.S.-China Relations.

Social Change: The Case of Rural China (Ezra Vogel, ed. Allyn & Bacon, Rockleigh, NJ 07647), was prepared by specialists under the auspices of the Committee on Sociological Resources for the Social Studies. Teacher's Guide and primary sources, $3.09. Highly recommended.

Other excellent curriculum materials are available from BAYCEP (Bay Area China Education Project, Stanford University, Stanford, CA 94305), and from most of the other centers listed under China and Asia Resource Centers in this guide.

Three periodicals dealing with religion in China are *China Notes*, a quarterly published by the China Program, National Council of Churches, 475 Riverside Drive, New York, NY 10115; *Tripod*, published by the Holy Spirit Study Centre, 6 Welfare Road, Aberdeen, Hong Kong; and *Bridge*, published by the Tao Fong Shan Ecumenical Centre, Box 33, Shatin, N.T., Hong Kong.

The best scholarly journal dealing with contemporary China is *The China Quarterly*, published by the Contemporary China Institute, School of Oriental and African Studies, London.

Three journals in English, published in China, are *Beijing Review*, a weekly journal of news and commentary; *China Pictorial* and *China Reconstructs*, both semi-popular journals with short articles and illustrations. These can be ordered through China Books & Periodicals, 2929 24th Street, San Francisco,

CA 94110. A free catalogue from China Books & Periodicals lists magazines, books, maps, posters, calendars, and crafts—most of them printed or produced in China.

The *U.S.–China Review* is a semi-popular journal, published six times a year by the U.S.–China Peoples Friendship Association, 100 Maryland Avenue, N.E., Washington, D.C. 20002.

Great Decisions, 1984 (Foreign Policy Association, 205 Lexington Avenue, New York, NY 10016) features eight topics, including "China & the U.S.—Five Years after Normalization." A Teacher's Guide and 24-page annotated bibliography are available on request. *A Supplement to Great Decisions, 1984*, explores the ethical values at stake, and is offered by the Council on Religion in International Affairs.

BOOKS

History and Culture of China

The most widely-used and respected overall survey is by John K. Fairbank, *The United States and China* (fourth edition, Harvard University Press, 1979).

Another good survey is by Lucian W. Pye, *China, An Introduction* (third edition, Little, Brown Company, 1984).

China Today

China Briefing (China Council of the Asia Society, 725 Park Avenue, New York, NY 10021), is an annual summary of the main events of the previous year; about 100 pages in length.

Values and Religion

In *The China Difference*, edited by Ross Terrill (Harper, 1979), sixteen China scholars present essays on a variety of topics, traditional and contemporary, all related to the subject of values.

Religion in Chinese Society by C. K. Yang (University of California Press, 1967), is the classic work describing the role of religion in Chinese society.

Chinese Religions by D. Howard Smith (Weidenfeld and Nicolson, 1968), is one of several scholarly books describing Chinese religions.

Religion in China by Robert G. Orr (Friendship Press, 1980), is a brief popular overview of Chinese religions, with over half the book devoted to the history of Christianity in China. The author updates his reporting to the year 1980.

Chinese Religion, An Introduction by Laurence G. Thompson (Wadsworth Press, 1979), is another good introductory survey.

Women and Family in China

Two excellent resources, prepared for secondary schools by the Minnesota Department of Education, provide reading selections and a teacher's guide. *Women in Traditional China* and *Women in Modern China* are available from GEM Publications, Inc., 411 Mallalieu Drive, Hudson, WI 54016. $3.95 each; Teacher's Guide $.95 each.

Women in China: Studies in Social Change and Feminism by Marilyn B. Young, ed. (Center for Chinese Studies, University of Michigan, 1973). A standard scholarly work.

The Chinese Family in the Communist Revolution by C. K. Yang (MIT Press, 1959), draws on the author's experience before and after 1949.

Village and Family in Contemporary China by William Parish, Jr., and Martin K. Whyte (University of Chicago Press, 1978),is a scholarly study based on interviews in Hong Kong.

Mao Zedong

Three books on Mao Zedong and his leadership in the Chinese Revolution are: *Mao: A Biography* by Ross Terrill (Harper and Row, 1980). *The People's Emperor: Mao* by Dick Wilson (Doubleday, 1980). *Mao's China: A History of the People's Republic of China* by Maurice Meisner (Free Press/Macmillan, 1977).

Robert Lifton's *Revolutionary Immortality: Mao Tse-tung and the Chinese Cultural Revolution* (Random House, 1968), is a fascinating analysis of campaign dynamics and revolutionary enthusiasm, by a psychiatrist.

Chinese Youth and the Meaning of Life

An entire issue of the quarterly journal *Chinese Education* (Spring 1981) is devoted to translations of letters from the Chinese monthly periodical *Chinese Youth* (Zhongguo Qingnian). M. E. Sharpe, 80 Business Park Drive, Armonk, NY 10504.

Coping with Death

An excellent resource and curriculum guide, *Dimensions of Loss and Death Education* by Patricia Weller Zalaznik, is published by Edu-Pac Co., P.O. Box 27101–B, Minneapolis, MN 55427. Two lessons are particularly relevant for this study: Lesson VII, "Values and Death," and Lesson VI, "Religious and Philosophical Viewpoints on Death."

See also, *Living and Dying* by Robert Lifton and Eric Olson (Praeger, 1974); *The Psychology of Death* by R. Kastenbaum and Ruth Aisenberg (Springer, 1972); and *The Denial of Death* by Ernest Becker (The Free Press, Macmillan, 1973).

Population, Food, and Resources

China and the World Food System by A. Doak Barnett (Overseas Development Council, 1979, 128 pages), is a concise, readable, and scholarly survey of China's agricultural policies and food production, in the context of the global food and population picture.

Food for One Billion: China's Agriculture Since 1949 by Robert Hsu (Westview Press, 1982, 125 pages), is an overview of agricultural policies and changes in China since 1949. It discusses how new policies and technology have enabled farm productivity to keep up with population growth.

China's Economy: A Basic Guide by Christopher Howe (Basic Books, 1978, 248 pages), is a survey for the non-specialist, by a well-known China scholar.

PRIMARY SOURCES FROM CHINA

The following books offer selected primary source materials, translated from the original Chinese.

The China Reader by Franz Schurmann and Orville Schell, eds. VOL. I: Imperial China, VOL. 2: Republican China; VOL. 3: Communist China; VOL. 4: People's China (New York: Vintage Books, paperback).

Through Chinese Eyes by Peter J. Seybolt, ed. VOL. 1: Revolution, A Nation Stands Up; VOL. 2: Transformation, Building a New Society (Center for International Training & Education, 777 United Nations Plaza, New York, NY 10017, revised edition, 1981, 160 pages each, Grades 9-12).

"What Is the Meaning of Life?" by Peter J. Seybolt, ed. Selections from *Chinese Youth* (Zhongguo Qingnian); in *Chinese Education* (a journal of translations) (M. E. Sharpe, Inc., 80 Business Park Drive, Armonk, NY 10504).

China Yesterday and Today (second edition) by Molly J. Coye and Jon Livingston, eds. (Bantam Books, Inc., 666 Fifth Avenue, New York, NY 10019).

Religious Policy and Practice in Communist China: A Documentary History by Donald MacInnis (New York and London, Macmillan, 1972). Selected writings, both official and unofficial, dealing with religion and religious policy in China.

Modern Chinese Stories by W. K. F. Jenner, ed. (Oxford, 1970, 271 pages). Short stories from 1900–1950 by several Chinese authors.

Dawn Blossoms Plucked at Dusk by Lu Hsun (Beijing, Foreign Languages Press, 1976, 92 pages). Ten satirical essays criticizing Confucian customs and the cruelty of the old society, by one of China's most famous writers.

Comrade Editor: Letters to the People's Daily by Hugh Thomas (Joint Publishers, 1980, 245 pages) is a selection of letters and editorials published in China's largest newspaper, revealing open criticism and complaints about many aspects of government policies and daily life.

AUDIO-VISUAL GUIDES AND RESOURCES

Most of the centers listed under China and Asia Resource Centers in this guide maintain audio-visual rental libraries, and will send listings on request.

Films from China are available from the four regional offices of the U.S.–China Peoples Friendship Association (USCPFA). A free catalogue is available from the national office, 2024 Eye Street, N.W., Suite 715, Washington, D.C. 20006.

The following audio-visual selections are recommended for supplementary use with Lessons 1 and 2 of *Focus On China*:

Perception/Misperceptions: China/United States is a set of three filmstrips with cassettes, student booklet, and teacher's guide, prepared by The Center for Global Perspectives. It includes: 1) "Images of Others" (a general introduction to stereotypes); 2) "Exploring Perceptions" (an introduction); and 3) "Through the Cultural Looking Glass" (Chinese and American cultural differences). It is available from: Prentice-Hall Media, 150 White Plains Road, Tarrytown, NY 10591.

Misunderstanding China is a widely-used film on American images of China, produced by CBS in 1972. Film footage is taken from old Charlie Chan movies, old films made in China, comic books, and other sources of American stereotypes of the Chinese. A teacher's guide with exercises and discussion has been prepared by BAYCEP at Stanford University (see China and Asian Resource Centers section following). The film is available from: U.S.–China People's Friendship Association, 720 Massachusetts Ave., Cambridge, MA 02139. Rental fee is $35, plus postage.

Looking at Us/Looking at Them is a show of 102 slides with cassette tapes that shows how images of people, often ludicrous, can be spread by films, comic books, and other popular media. The show comes in two sets: Part 1, "Looking for China: American Images"; and Part 2, "Looking for America: Chinese Images." It is available for purchase only for $15 each part, from: China Council, The Asia Society, 725 Park Ave., New York, NY 10021.

CHINA AND ASIA RESOURCE CENTERS

Listed are twenty-four centers that offer program and resource assistance to secondary schools. Services include newsletters, curriculum units, speakers, and audio-visual materials. Most of these are regional, but two serve national constituencies. These are:

The Center for Teaching About China
U.S.–China People's Friendship Association
110 Maryland Avenue, N.E.
Washington, D.C. 20002.

Education Department
The Asia Society
725 Park Avenue
New York, NY 10021

The following are Regional Centers:

Arizona

Asian Resource Center
The East Asia Center
204 Selim Franklin Building
University of Arizona
Tucson, Arizona 85721

California

Bay Area China Education Project
(BAYCEP)
Stanford University
Stanford, CA 94305

Connecticut

Outreach Program
Council on East Asian Studies
Yale University
Box 13A, Yale Station
85 Trumbull Street
New Haven, CT 06520

Illinois

Center for Asian Studies
1208 West California
University of Illinois, Urbana-Champaign
Urbana, IL 61801

Massachusetts

East Asian Program
Harvard University/Children's Museum
Museum Wharf
300 Congress Street
Boston, MA 02210

Five College Center for East Asian Studies
Thompson Hall 110
University of Massachusetts
Amherst, MA 01003

Michigan

Project on East Asian Studies in Education (PEASE)
108 Lane Hall
University of Michigan
Ann Arbor, Michigan 48109

Minnesota

Schools Outreach Program
Midwest China Center
308 Gullixson Hall
2375 Como Avenue West
St. Paul, MN 55108

New Jersey

Department of East Asian Studies
Princeton University
211 Jones Hall
Princeton, NJ 08540

New York

East Asian Curriculum Project (EACP)
East Asian Institute
Columbia University
420 West 118th Street
New York, NY 10027

Asian Studies Curriculum Center
New York University
735 East Building
Washington Square
New York, NY 10003

Ohio

School and Community Outreach Program on Asia
(SCOPA)
East Asian Studies Program
The Ohio State University
308 Dulles Hall, 230 West 17th Avenue
Columbus, OH 43210

East Asian Studies Outreach Program
King 141
Oberlin College
Oberlin, OH 44074

Pennsylvania

East Asian Studies Center
University Center for International Studies
4E38 Forbes Quadrangle
University of Pittsburgh
Pittsburgh, PA 15260

Texas

TEXPERA (Texas Program for Educational Resources
on Asia)
Center for Asian Studies
SSB 4.126
University of Texas at Austin
Austin, TX 78712

Utah

BYU ASIA
Asia in Schools for Intercultural Action
134 FOB
Brigham Young Unversity
Provo, UT 84602

Virginia

East Asia Language and Area Center
University of Virginia
1644 Oxford Road
Charlottesville, VA 22903

Washington

East Asia Resource Center (EARC)
School of International Studies
302C Thomson Hall
University of Washington
Seattle, WA 98195

MARYKNOLL IN BRIEF

Maryknoll is the overseas heart and hands of the Catholic Church in America. Founded in 1911 as The Catholic Foreign Mission Society of America, Maryknoll is the instrument through which American Catholics reach out to their brothers and sisters in other lands and other cultures.

Maryknollers share the Gospel, not in words alone, but in practical and concrete actions: by feeding the hungry, clothing the naked, providing shelter for the homeless, caring for the sick, and accompanying the poor and oppressed in their struggles.

Over 950 Maryknoll Priests, Associate Priests, Brothers, Lay Missioners and Seminarians use their diverse talents and skills to serve God's poor in twenty-seven countries. Their mission work includes sacramental ministry, community development, teaching, public health, farming, refugee work, lay leadership development, and orphanage administration.

Respecting the rich culture of the peoples they serve, Maryknollers make every effort to develop Christian communities and encourage a native Catholic clergy. The missioners' goal is to awaken the hope and knowledge of Christ in other peoples, to show the Holy Spirit at work in every culture.